Come Unto Me

Resting in the Favor Of the King

Tania Frankie

iUniverse, Inc.
New York Lincoln Shanghai

Come Unto Me
Resting in the Favor of the King

Copyright © 2008 by Tania Lee Frankie

All rights reserved. No part of this book may be used or reproduced by any means, graphic, electronic, or mechanical, including photocopying, recording, taping or by any information storage retrieval system without the written permission of the publisher except in the case of brief quotations embodied in critical articles and reviews.

iUniverse books may be ordered through booksellers or by contacting:

iUniverse
2021 Pine Lake Road, Suite 100
Lincoln, NE 68512
www.iuniverse.com
1-800-Authors (1-800-288-4677)

Because of the dynamic nature of the Internet, any Web addresses or links contained in this book may have changed since publication and may no longer be valid.

The views expressed in this work are solely those of the author and do not necessarily reflect the views of the publisher, and the publisher hereby disclaims any responsibility for them.

ISBN: 978-0-595-44886-9 (pbk)
ISBN: 978-0-595-71118-5 (cloth)
ISBN: 978-0-595-89209-9 (ebk)

Printed in the United States of America

Come Unto Me is a listening post to the living voice of a loving heavenly Father who deeply desires an intimacy with us. In these devotional readings, you will come face to face with the personal God of the Scriptures, the Father of Jesus who speaks words of encouragement, instruction, life and hope into your life. In each, you will feel yourself personally addressed. In each, the heavenly Father will open His heart to you as He draws you into His very presence. I predict you will return to these readings time and again.

Pastor David N. Glesne

Unless otherwise indicated, all Scripture quotations are taken from the Holy Bible, New King James Version. Copyright 1979, 1980, 1982 by Thomas Nelson, Inc.

Scripture quotations marked (NLT) are taken from the Holy Bible, New living translation, copyright 1996. Used by permission of Tyndale House Publishers, Inc, Wheaton, Illinois 60189. All rights reserved.

Scripture quotations marked (NIV) are taken from the HOLY BIBLE, NEW INTERNATIONAL VERSION, NIV. Copyright 1973, 1978, 1984, by International Bible Society. Used by permission of Zondervan. All rights reserved.

All illustrations by Brandon Kidder, inhisnamebk@hotmail.com

I dedicate this book to the LORD.
May it give Him glory
And bless many.

Contents

Preface xiii
Acknowledgments xv

Dwell In Me 2
I Am So Near 4
I Am Real 6
Choose The One Thing That Is Needed 7
You Are Beautifully Unique 9

Enter My Rest 12
You Have Everything You Need 14
Let Me Define You 16
Let My Light Shine 18

My Grace Is Sufficient 22
It's Not Too Late 24
You Are Completely Forgiven 25
I Identify With You 27
Be Free 29
My Love Is Blind 31
Love Begets Love 33

Savor Your Savior 36
You Are My Reward 38
I Hold Out My Scepter For You 40
You Were Not Created To Serve Me 42
You Are My Friend 44

Judge Not 48
The Truth Shall Set You Free 50
In Whom Do You Confide? 54
Abide In My Love 56

Right Here, Right Now 62
Who Are You Believing? 63
I Am Trustworthy, Even In Your Affliction 65
Let Me Be Your Relief 68
The Whole Picture 70

What Can Possibly Harm You? 74
Press On 76
Know Who You Are 77
Let Me Be Your Portion 79
Are You Willing To Run? 81

Know The Joy Of Submitting To My Authority 84
Receive My Love, Then Pass It On To Others 86
I Am Still Involved 89
Choose Me 92

Faith Without Works Is Dead 96
Look Unto Me 98
Do Not Settle For Less Than Me 100
My Heart's Desire 102
Do Not Settle Into The Status Quo 104

What Are You Clinging To? 108
Seek Not The Kingdom Of This World 110
What Do You Seek? 112
Come To Me 114

Be Yourself 118
All That Is Beautiful 119
You Are My Beloved 120
My Treasure 122

Preface

Come Unto Me is the result of time spent sitting at the Lord's feet in the midst of life's joys and struggles. It is the result of seeking His heart and wisdom in a world full of conflicting ideas, philosophies, opinions, and beliefs. It is the ministering of His Spirit, who illumines truth, hope, peace, and joy.

Allow the meditations in this book to touch your heart. Take your time, pondering the truth, depth, and meaning of each verse of Scripture. Listen for the Lord's gentle whisper inviting you to come closer. Be still, and enjoy the fellowship of His loving presence.

Whether you are researching the validity of faith in Christ, or have walked with Him in intimate maturity, you will be touched by the love of the Lord and irresistibly drawn to His side.

May you be blessed as your journey with the Lord continues. May you be refreshed with the joy of His presence. May you revel in His gentle whisper as you draw closer and closer to Him. And may you rest in the sweetness of His favor.

Acknowledgments

Thank you, Pastor David Glesne, for blessing me with your time in the midst of a schedule I know is busy. You supported and encouraged me all the way through the process to the finish line. This book was completed, in large part, because of your cheers from the balcony.

Thank you, Diane Larson, for all the time and effort you put into editing, offering suggestions, and checking references. I so appreciate everything you taught me. Your enthusiasm, support, and willingness to help mean more than I can say. I'm so blessed that you're my sister.

Karen Thomas, your prayers, support, editing suggestions, and friendship have been rich blessings. I'm so grateful for you. Thank you for everything.

Brandon Kidder, your art has blessed my heart and this book. Thank you so much for praying and partnering with me on such a wonderful adventure.

Judy and Bill Kidder, I'm humbled by your support, prayers, and enthusiasm. Thank you so much. What rich blessings you are!

*"But whoever drinks
Of the water
That I shall give him
Will never thirst.
But the water that I
Shall give him will
Become in him a
Fountain of water
Springing up into
Everlasting life."*
John 4:14

Dwell In Me

The beloved of the LORD shall dwell in safety by Him, Who shelters him all the day long; And he shall dwell between His shoulders.
Dt 33:12

My beloved, I want you to dwell continuously between My shoulders with your ears inclined to My heart. This is where you will find shelter from the storms of life (Ps 61:3-4). This is where you will find great peace and joy (Isa 26:3-4). This is where you will know I am your sufficiency (2 Co 3:5), strength (Ps 118:14), protector (Ps 34:7, 91:1-2, 94:18), provider (Jn 14:13-14), Savior (Jn 4:42), beloved (SS 2:16), and friend (Jn 15:13-15). This is where you will learn that I am indeed good (Ps 34:8), trustworthy (Ps 9:10), and faithful (Dt 7:9, 1 Co 1:9). This is where you will learn about My great love for you. This is where you will learn to rest in My continuous favor.

Dwelling in My presence, every moment of every day, no matter what you are doing, is My desire for your life (Mic 6:8). I created you to have a loving relationship with Me (Mt 22:36-38). In order to walk in that relationship, you need to set aside time to spend with Me.

How I long for you, My precious one, to be in My arms, leaning your head against My chest, listening to the beat of My heart for you: for I love you, even unto death (Jn 15:13).

You say you want to know Me better and that you want a greater revelation of Me and My love. You say you want a deeper awareness of My presence in your life. Then spend time with Me. Turn toward Me. Realize that I am the One who wants these things for you even more than you want them for yourself. Isn't spending time with people how you get to know them? Isn't that what revelation is—getting to know someone better and better? So spend time with Me, and I will give you the desires of your heart (Ps 37:4).

How I miss you when you choose not to spend time with Me. How I miss you when you are not in My arms. Seek Me, and you will find Me, but you need to seek (Lk 11:9).

When you are in My arms, you will find there is absolutely no need to strive. All you have to do is choose to remain in My arms, resting in My favor, and I will provide everything you need: I will transform you more and more into My likeness (2 Co 3:18, Php 1:6). I will give you the gifts and talents you need to fulfill your call (2 Co 9:8, Php 4:19). I will guide you, show you the way, and provide for you (Ps 23:1-3). I will remind you that you are forgiven and free (Mk 3:28, Jn 8:36, 1 Jn 2:12). I will remind you that you do not need to prove yourself in an attempt to earn My love and affection (Ro 5:8). I will teach you how to let go and rest in My favor.

I will soothe and comfort you (Ps 94:19). I will hide and protect you from the enemy who would seek to snatch you from My arms (Jn 10:28-29). I will remind you there is no need for striving of any sort. For when you are in My arms, I am the One who is accomplishing everything as you remain yielded to Me (Eph 3:20). I will teach you that there is never a moment when you are not welcome in My arms—no matter what you are going through, and no matter what you are thinking or feeling (Eph 2:13). I will be your All and your Everything—your Alpha and your Omega (Rev 22:13), and you will discover there is no greater peace, joy, or strength than when you are abiding and resting in My arms (Jn 14:27).

So come, My beloved, and rest your head against My chest. Learn to stay in this sweet embrace continuously no matter what you are doing or where you are going. Rest in My complete and all-sufficient provision for every single physical, mental, emotional, and spiritual need you have. Stay in My arms listening to My heart and you will have everything you need to fight the good fight (1 Ti 6:12), to run the good race (Heb 12:1), and to work out your salvation daily (Php 2:12). Remember, apart from Me you can do nothing (Jn 15:5), but in My loving embrace you can indeed do all things (Mt 19:26).

I Am So Near

Be still and know that I am God.
Ps 46:10

My precious child, I know there are times when you are frustrated because you want to have a greater awareness of My loving presence in your life. Beloved, I want to give you the desires of your heart (Ps 37:4); I want you to know and experience My nearness and great love for you as you go about your day.

The secret is this: be still. Remember, I am not in the wind, the earthquake, or the fire. I am not in the rush of activity, noise, and chaos of life. I am the still small voice that whispers deep within your heart (1 Ki 19:11-13).

However, do not misunderstand Me, My love, for I am with you always (Mt 28:20), including when your life is full of activity, noise, and chaos. But you need to be still, quiet yourself, and intentionally set aside time to listen for My still small voice. As you learn to focus on Me in the quietness of your prayer closet (Mt 6:6), you will gradually learn to focus on Me throughout the rest of your day. But you need to be diligent in intentionally setting time apart to meet with Me in stillness (Dt 4:29, Jer 29:13, Heb 11:6). Then, once you've developed an increased awareness of My loving presence for you throughout the day, you will discover there is no time so sweet as when we meet together in stillness and quiet intimacy (Ps 65:4, 84:1-2, 10).

My beloved Son knew this well (Mt 26:36, Lk 5:16, 6:12). He often sent His closest companions away, so He could meet with Me in quiet intimacy (Mt 14:22-23). You need to do the same, My child, following your beloved Savior's example.

If you do not feel there is any time left in your busy schedule for quietness with Me, ask Me to show you where the imbalance is, and I will surely show you. If you struggle with not being motivated to be still, ask Me to give you that desire. If you struggle with a lack of focus, with your mind wandering in many different directions as you try to wait upon Me, ask Me to help you. I will surely answer all these prayers and more (Mt 7:7-11). Remember, I am the Source of every good gift (Jas 1:17), and you have not, because you ask not (Jas 4:2).

Be persistent, My child, and you *will* experience My reward (Lk 18:1-8). But you must persist, refusing to give up before receiving everything I have promised you. If you find your solitude with Me feeling empty and dry, ask yourself if you are sitting quietly out of obligation, so you can check it off your spiritual discipline "to do" list, or if you are really being still with the desire to meet with the Person who loves you beyond knowledge (Eph 3:19). Remember, all spiritual disciplines—prayer, fasting, reading My Word, and the like—serve to connect you with Me. They are never an end in themselves.

So delight yourself in Me, not in the disciplines, and I will give you the desires of your heart (Ps 37:4). I *will* meet with you. I *will* give you an awareness of My sweet presence. I *will* give you an awareness of the love I lavish upon you (1 Jn 3:1). I *will* speak to you and meet with you (Jn 10:27). You will learn that I still speak through visions, dreams, thoughts, and impressions (Joel 2:28). You will learn that I *love* your attention. I *love* interacting with you. I *love* sharing with you, and I *love* telling you the secrets of My heart (Ps 25:14, Isa 45:3, Da 2:22).

So be still, beloved, and enter into a deeper, more profound relationship with Me than you ever imagined. Be still, and discover that there is none like Me (Isa 45:5). Be still and know.

I Am Real

"I AM WHO I AM."
Ex 3:14

*M*y precious child, I want you to know, deeply and profoundly, that I am real; I am more real and permanent than anything you can see, taste, smell, hear, or touch (2 Co 4:18). The kingdom of this world will soon pass away. However, My kingdom is permanent, everlasting, and will never pass away (1 Jn 2:17, Rev 21:1-3); My kingdom is real and eternal and so am I (1 Ti 1:17).

Won't you choose that which will never pass away? O how I want to be more real to you than anything else (1 Jn 5:20).

My beloved, in order to grow into a deep and profound awareness of how real I am, you need to seek Me (Dt 4:29, 2 Ch 15:2b, Lk 11:9). You need to look beyond that which you can see with the natural eye and hear with the natural ear (Ro 8:24-25, 2 Co 5:7). You need to seek *Me*.

For now you see through a glass dimly (1 Co 13:12), but I will be revealed to you more and more as you seek to gaze upon My face. The more you seek, the more I will be revealed (2 Co 9:6, Gal 6:7-8), until that glorious day when you finally see Me face to face.

You need to remember that seeking is not a one-time event. Do not satisfy yourself with the glimmer of understanding and revelation you currently have, for I am infinite, and I am infinitely beautiful and wonderful to behold (Job 37:22, Ps 27:4, 93:1). I am real (Isa 43:10-11). I am deep (Ps 92:5, 1 Co 2:10). I am mysterious (Mt 13:11, 1 Co 4:1). I am great (Ps 48:1), and I can be found (Jer 29:13).

So seek Me, beloved. Enter into My presence daily, growing in knowledge and understanding. Then I will make you strong in spirit. I will fill you with wisdom. I will surround you with grace (Lk 2:40), and you will know that I am real.

<u>Choose The One Thing That Is Needed</u>

*Now it happened as they went that He entered a certain village; and a certain woman named Martha welcomed Him into her house. And she had a sister called Mary, who also sat at Jesus' feet and heard His word. But Martha was distracted with much serving, and she approached Him and said, "Lord, do You not care that my sister has left me to serve alone? Therefore tell her to help me." And Jesus answered and said to her, "Martha, Martha, you are worried and troubled about many things. But **one thing** (emphasis mine) is needed, and Mary has chosen that good part, which will not be taken away from her."*
Lk 10:38-42

My beloved, do you see what is needed? Do you understand what is important? Will you choose that which is good?

How I long for you to choose to sit at My feet. I know this defies the world's standards of productivity and wisdom. However, you need to remember that My ways are not your ways (Isa 55:8-9), and the wisdom of this world is foolishness in My eyes (1 Co 3:18-20).

Take note, My child, of the many cultural norms and rules Mary chose to defy as she determined to sit at My feet: In her day it was expected of her to wait on the men in the house offering them food and drink. To neglect this duty was considered impolite at best and insulting to the male guests at worst. Yet My precious Mary chose the *one thing* that was needed—the good part; she chose to sit at My feet.

Mary's culture was such that it was unheard of for a lone woman to linger in the presence of a room full of men. This would have been considered highly inappropriate, a blow to her good reputation, an affront to the authority of men, and a rebellion against what was considered to be her inferior status. Yet My precious Mary chose the *one thing* that was needed—the good part; she chose to sit at My feet.

Mary's sister, Martha, considered her rude and lazy as she chose to sit at My feet. Yet Mary chose Me in spite of her sister's disapproval. My precious Mary chose the *one thing* that was needed—the good part; she chose to sit at My feet.

What is the world telling you that you must value and thus choose above spending time at My feet? Is it your job, ministry, family, responsibilities in the home, television, newspaper, or your favorite team? Or do you fear what others will think if you spend time with Me—risking the stigma of laziness and lack of contribution?

Do not misunderstand, My child, I am not calling you to turn your back on your responsibilities. However, I am calling you to turn your eyes toward the one needful thing—seeking first the good part—while knowing and believing that everything else will be added unto you (Mt 6:33).

So, make time for Me. Choose the one thing that is needed. Seek first My kingdom and My righteousness instead of the ways of the world, and everything else will fall into place. I created you to enjoy fellowship with Me (1 Co 1:9). So do not let the distractions and norms of your culture rob you of the joy of sitting at My feet.

Simply choose the good part—the *one thing* that is needed.

You Are Beautifully Unique

Yes, the body has many different parts, not just one part. If the foot says, "I am not a part of the body because I am not a hand," that does not make it any less a part of the body. And if the ear says, "I am not part of the body because I am only an ear and not an eye," would that make it any less a part of the body? Suppose the whole body were an eye—then how would you hear? Or if your whole body were just one big ear, how could you smell anything? But God made our bodies with many parts, and He has put each part just where He wants it. What a strange thing a body would be if it had only one part! Yes, there are many parts, but only one body. The eye can never say to the hand, "I don't need you." The head can't say to the feet, "I don't need you."
1 Co 12:14-21, NLT

Beloved, you need to fully realize how much I cherish you as a wonderfully unique individual. How often you have looked at others and wished you had a quality or trait that was uniquely theirs. My child, you need to trust that when I look at you—your personality, your abilities, all that makes you beautifully unique—I smile and say, "It is very good" (Ge 1:31).

I created you for a very specific purpose (Jn 15:16, Eph 2:10). And in My wisdom, love, and provision, I have given you everything you need to fulfill your unique call (2 Co 9:8, Php 4:19). I have given you all the beautiful, unique qualities that make you who you are. So you see, I am the One who encourages you and calls you forth to be all you are meant to be—in all your unique beauty.

I am also the One who transforms those parts of you that do not reflect who I created you to be. However, there is a vast difference between the transformation I work within you so that you become more and more like Me (Php 1:6) and accepting who you are as a unique individual. I transform you from glory to glory (2 Co 3:18). However, I do this while absolutely cherishing and delighting in you and all that makes you unique and beautiful.

So do not despise your own matchless beauty, worth, and loveliness, because I delight in all these things about you. After all, I am the One who has blessed you with those characteristics. They will enable you to fulfill your call as you abide in Me (Jn 15:4-5, Php 4:13). So come, My love, and be delighted in the unique qualities I have given you. In this way you will be mirroring My delight in you and blessing My heart with your thankfulness and joy.

*For without Me
You can do
Nothing.*
John 15:5

Enter My Rest

Therefore, since a promise remains of entering His rest, let us fear lest any of you seem to have come short of it. For we who have believed do enter that rest. Let us therefore be diligent to enter that rest, lest anyone fall according to the same example of disobedience.
Heb 4:1,3, 11

My precious one, come and enter My rest. My rest that produces a peace far beyond anything the world has to offer (Jn 14:27). My rest that comes from entrusting to Me all that is you—your talents, flaws, gifts, emotions, mind, body, heart, desires, dreams, ministry, family, and possessions. All that you are, all that you have, and all that you endeavor to be needs to be surrendered to Me (Ro 12:1-2). Won't you trust Me to fulfill everything I have promised you? For when you trust in Me, in My promises, and in My love for you, surrendering everything becomes possible.

You've tried so hard to become more like Me, to do what is right, to bring forth My kingdom here on earth, to produce lasting fruit, to refrain from sin, and to make yourself "good enough" to please Me. Don't you know that all this striving is for naught even though you struggle toward a noble goal? My beloved and precious child, do not fall short of My rest due to fleshly striving that stems from unbelief and disobedience.

Beloved, put down all your striving and come unto Me—your gentle and humble Teacher—and I will give you rest (Mt 11:28-30). All you need to do is come to Me as you are, trusting that I will fulfill everything I have promised. Remember, I promise, that as you look to Me, *I* will transform you more and more into My image (2 Co 3:17-19). So stop striving to transform yourself, and let Me do what I have promised.

My precious one, you need to take your eyes off yourself and put them on Me. You need to die to yourself, die to trying to do that which only I can do, die to all your striving, and let Me resurrect it all so that you can produce much fruit (Jn 12:24). Stop trying so hard to produce fruit by your own efforts. Instead, simply believe that when you remain in Me and I in you, you *will* bear much fruit. Remember, I tell you that you can do nothing apart from Me (Jn 15:4-5). Who, then, is producing the fruit—you striving to produce something to please Me, or you abiding in Me and allowing Me to transform you into a fruit-bearing branch?

Submit, obey, trust, and believe, and *I* will bring forth the fruit in you. Then give Me thanks and praise for continuing to accomplish the good work I began within you (Php 1:6). Remember, nothing good can come from your fleshly striving (Ro 7:18), because whatever is good and perfect comes from Me alone (Jas 1:16-18). I am the Source of all that is good. It's about Me and My power at work within you. It's about Me receiving the glory for that which I am doing in and through you (Eph 3:20-21). I am the Source, My beloved. I am the Source (Ro 11:36)!

So be diligent, My child, to die to your striving and to "let go and let God," lest you be tempted to boast in your own efforts (Eph 2:8-9). For in turning your gaze upon Me and resting in My promises—not in struggling in your own efforts—you will be saved (Isa 30:15a). And in quiet confidence and trust in Me, you will find strength (Isa 30:15b).

So come and rest in Me, beloved. Step aside. Allow Me to do everything I have promised, trusting in My love, goodness, timing, and wisdom, to accomplish much more than anything you would ask or think (Eph 3:20). Enter My rest. Cease from striving. Trust in Me, and taste and see that I am good (Ps 34:8).

You Have Everything You Need

You both precede and follow me. You place your hand of blessing on my head. Such knowledge is too wonderful for me, too great for me to know! I can never escape from Your spirit! I can never get away from Your presence! If I go up to heaven, You are there; if I go down to the place of the dead, You are there. If I ride the wings of the morning, if I dwell by the farthest oceans, even there Your hand will guide me, and Your strength will support me. I could ask darkness to hide me and the light around me to become night—but even in darkness I cannot hide from You. To You the night shines as bright as day. Darkness and light are both alike to You.
Ps 139:5-12, NLT

My beloved, I want you to realize there is no need to strive, to cling, to hang on to, to obtain, or to grasp Me or any of My blessings.

I tell you this because there have been times when you've worked so hard to hang onto that which you can never lose. Do you see that *I* am the One who holds onto *you*? *I* am the One who precedes and follows you. *I* am the One who will never leave you (Heb 13:5). *I* am the One who guides you and gives you My strength and support. *I* am the One who will be by your side no matter what you are thinking and feeling, and no matter how much you are struggling with sin and darkness. Do you understand, now, that there isn't a time, place, or situation in which I am not with you and caring for you?

Now do you see that you have no need to frantically hold onto Me, fearing if you let go you will lose Me? *I* am the One who is holding onto *you*! I am the One who is keeping you safely in the palm of My hand (Ps 37:23-24, 95:7, Jn 10:28). This means you do not have to struggle to remain in My grasp. You're already there. Be still and know, My beloved. Be still and know (Ps 46:10). Fear not, little one, for I am with you even unto the end of time (Mt 28:20), and there's nothing you can do to change that.

Do you see what this means, My love? Let him who has ears listen and understand. *I* am the One who places My hand of blessing upon you. You don't have to strain and strive to receive My blessings; I simply give them to you. I *love* caring for you. I *love* blessing you; it is My *good pleasure* to give you My kingdom (Lk 12:32)!

This means you do not need to desperately cling to My salvation; it's yours. You do not need to struggle to hold onto My grace; it's yours. You do not need to grasp for My protection; it's yours. You do not need to hunt for My provision; it's yours: for you are in My hand, and I place all My blessings upon you. Such knowledge truly is too great and too wonderful to fully comprehend.

Rejoice, and be free from your hunting, striving, grasping, and worrying about obtaining something that is already yours. Live in freedom, My love, for you are free indeed (Jn 8:36). Rest in My provision. Rest in My favor. Rest in My grace. Rest in My love. Rest in My steadfastness and faithfulness. Though you may be experiencing changes in circumstances, shifts in feelings, struggles with sin and darkness, storms of doubt, and battles within your mind, *I never change* (Heb 13:8): My provision for you never changes. My love for you never changes. My grace for you never changes. And the fact that you're in My hand never changes.

So rest in these truths: You have made Me your shelter. You have invited Me into your life. You have chosen to follow Me. You desire to obey Me; that's all that matters.

I know your heart. The fact that you struggle with sin does not change the fact that I am holding you. I sent My Son to embrace sinners, to embrace the ones who would choose Me (Mk 2:17). You have responded to My embrace. I do the rest. You reside in My shelter. I am your refuge, your place of safety, and the One who holds you in the palm of My hand.

Now do you understand that you already have everything you need? Rejoice, My child, for you are completely surrounded by Me. That means that you are completely surrounded by My love, grace, provision, protection, and so much more. I love you, My child, and I would have it no other way.

Let Me Define You

The next day a great multitude that had come to the feast, when they heard that Jesus was coming to Jerusalem, took branches of palm trees and went out to meet Him, and cried out: "Hosanna! 'Blessed is He who comes in the name of the LORD!' The King of Israel!"
Jn 12:12
Pilate answered and said to them again, "What then do you want me to do with Him whom you call the King of the Jews?" So they cried out again, "Crucify Him!" Then Pilate said to them, "Why, what evil has He done?" But they cried out all the more, "Crucify Him!"
Mk 15:12-14

My beloved child, let Me define you. Let Me be the One you look to for the truth of your value and worth. Do not look to other's reactions to you, or opinions of you, in an effort to feel valued or worthy. Do not look to others for praise and affirmation in order to feel accepted and loved (Pr 29:5). Also, do not succumb to feelings of shame or condemnation (Ro 8:1) just because others are angry or disappointed with you. Beloved, I do not even want *you* to try to determine your own worth; for your worth, My precious child, can only be determined by My immeasurable love for you (Jn 15:13, 1 Jn 4:9-11).

Look at what happened to My Son. Do you see how He would have suffered needlessly if He had based His worth on the reactions of the multitudes? One moment the multitudes love Him and are worshipping and honoring Him. The next moment they have completely turned against Him, ridiculing Him, shouting, "Crucify Him!" Do you see the turmoil that results in letting others determine whether you are truly loved and valued? One moment you're loved and accepted. The next moment you're hated and rejected. However, do the fickle alliances of others really reflect or determine your worth? Of course not!

Let Me define your worth. Let Me satisfy you with My everlasting love and acceptance as you abide in Me (Jer 31:3). Keep Me as your Lord by looking to *Me* for the truth of your value and worth. Do not focus on the opinions of others or even on your opinions about yourself; I want you to focus on who *I* say you are. What I'm saying is, do not let your opinions or the opinions of others become your idol (Ps 118:8).

My Son was secure in the knowledge that His value and worth were not dependent upon what others thought of Him. In fact, He made a lot of people angry because He would not bend to their desires and demands (Jn 6:64, 7:1). He knew there was a much higher calling on His life than simply fulfilling the wants and needs of those around Him. He also understood that His love for others never diminished or wavered, even when He chose not to comply with their wishes. Oftentimes, My child, love says, "No."

Remember, it is often appropriate and necessary to say "no"—even to legitimate wants and needs. My Son had to send multitudes of people away, even though they wanted to spend more time with Him (Mt 15:39). However, sending them away was not an indication of His lack of love or concern for them. And it does not mean you do not love others when you say, "No."

Consider, My beloved, the prophets of old: most were hated, judged, rejected, and even killed, because they didn't give others what they wanted. However, *I* was well pleased with them. I was pleased because they chose to follow Me rather than seeking the approval of others (Mt 5:11-12).

So, remember, I did not create you to please others by walking in *their* ways (Ro 12:2). I created you to abide in Me and walk in *My* ways (Pr 3:5-6, Isa 55:8-9). I created you to live an abundant life (Jn 10:10): abiding forever in My loving presence and knowing your tremendous value in My eyes. I also created you, so I can enjoy your presence as you walk with Me.

So be at peace, My child, for you are not called to please anyone but Me. And rejoice, for I am the One who defines you. I alone determine your worth. And you are of immeasurable worth simply because of My immeasurable love for you (1 Jn 3:1).

Let My Light Shine

Most assuredly, I say to you, unless a grain of wheat falls into the ground and dies, it remains alone; but if it dies, it produces much grain.
Jn 12:24
But we have this treasure in earthen vessels, that the excellence of the power may be of God and not of us.
2 Co 4:7

My dear one, you must stop investing yourself in all that you do. Instead, I want you to die to yourself; I want you to stop relying on your own power and efforts so that *My* power can be manifested through you (Gal 2:20).

Do not fall into the trap of believing that what you do represents who you are, or that who you are is connected to what you do. You are not defined by what you do—whether that be caring for your family, maintaining a career, or serving Me in any other way; I created you to be a human *being*, not a human *doing*.

There are so many who believe in the value of pouring one's heart into whatever they are doing. Your culture teaches that pouring one's heart into an activity somehow improves the outcome, producing a higher quality result. The kingdom of this world values this kind of pouring out and highly encourages it.

However, My love, the only thing I want you to pour your heart into is Me. I want you to fully recognize that whatever abilities you have are from Me. I want you to understand that pouring yourself into the gift, ability, or talent I have given you does not improve upon the gift. In fact, pouring your heart into anything to the point of defining yourself by that activity or gift is harmful. You are a child of the Most High God (1 Jn 3:1), not a child of the *gifts* of the Most High God.

I want to work through you more powerfully than you can ever imagine (Eph 3:20-21). However, I can't work through you as powerfully as I would like if you insist on placing so much of yourself in the gifts I have given you. Instead, I want you to step aside, and leave *Me* room to manifest *My* power.

Do you see the freedom in this, My love? You are *not* the gifts and abilities I have given you: Your value is not reflected in how developed these gifts are. You are not one with the gifts. You are not defined by the gifts. You are also not responsible for the outcome when you use the gifts. You are only responsible to steward the gifts well—to use them when and how I tell you.

This means that when you are not as accomplished in using your gifts as you would like, you need not feel ashamed. This is because I am not looking for perfection. I just want you to use your gifts when I tell you to do so. However, do not misunderstand, I do want you to grow, develop, and learn how to use your gifts; that is a part of being a good steward. But, in that process of growing and learning, I want you to trust Me to work through you: I want you to stop striving in your own efforts. I want you to stop pouring yourself into your gifts in an effort to attain a desired outcome, and I want you to step out of the way. Only then can I receive glory as I manifest My power through you.

Consider Jeremiah. I gave him a powerful prophetic gift, but he was *not* the gift itself: He did not define himself by his gift. He did not pour his heart into the gift to try to improve upon it, and did he take pride in the fact that he was using his gift well. He simply prophesied as I directed him, making no effort to control the outcome. In fact, I told him that when he prophesied people would hate him, wouldn't listen to him, and would even try to kill him (Jer 18:18-20). Yet he chose to obey, stewarding well the gift I had given him.

He chose to obey. That's all. He died to himself and became an empty vessel so that My power could be manifested through him. And although others hated him for being obedient, I was *well pleased* (Mt 5:11-12).

So, My beloved, stop striving. Stop pouring your heart into the gifts I have given you. Instead, die to your own efforts to produce; step aside, and let Me manifest My power through you. Don't concern yourself with how you are perceived by others when you utilize your gifts. Don't berate yourself when you believe you have not performed well.

Remember, I am not looking for perfection—just obedience; I'm looking for someone who is willing to step aside, and let My light shine.

*Therefore if the Son
Makes you
Free,
You shall be
Free indeed.*
John 8:36

My Grace Is Sufficient

Who shall bring a charge against God's elect? It is God who justifies. Who is he who condemns? It is Christ who died, and furthermore is also risen, who is even at the right hand of God, who also makes intercession for us. Who shall separate us from the love of Christ? Shall tribulation, or distress, or persecution, or famine, or nakedness, or peril, or sword?
Ro 8:33-35
Yet in all these things we are more than conquerors through Him who loved us.
Ro 8:37

My child, do you realize these verses pertain both to your past and your present? Do you realize this means there is absolutely no reason to succumb to condemnation for *any* failure, shortcoming, or sin? Do you realize this means that, because you have turned to Me, you are on the right path no matter how many wrong turns you may have taken in the past? For when you walk with Me, humbly confessing your sins, you *are* on the right path: You are being sanctified. You are becoming more and more like Me. You are learning to trust and love Me. You are learning to walk in My will—and that's all that matters.

I want you to realize this means you can let go of all the "if onlys" in your life. "If only I had become a Christian sooner, I would have become something better for the Lord, chosen a different career, lived somewhere else, helped more people ..." Rejoice, My precious one, for My grace really is sufficient, and My strength is made perfect in your weakness (2 Co 12:9).

Think upon this amazing truth and promise: all your weaknesses, sins, poor decisions, wrong turns, brokenness, and insufficiencies are covered by My *all sufficient grace*, and by My strength to make your crooked paths straight (Lk 3:5-6). This is the power of My blood shed for you on the cross. This is the depth of My love for you.

Remember, I did not come into the world to condemn it; I came to save it (Jn 3:17-18). I also came so you would have abundant life (Jn 10:10). Do not let the thief steal your abundance by listening to and believing his accusations against you. Who dares accuse those whom I Myself have justified?

Rejoice, My child! You are free from the accuser who condemns you over and over for the sin in your life. You are free from the struggle and torment of trying to make up or pay for your sins. Remember, I already *paid-in-full* the price for your sinfulness. Your debt is paid—completely erased *forever*! In its place I have given you salvation, strength, and the kingdom of God. My power has cast down the accuser. I have overcome him with My blood (Rev 12:10-11). Now there is only grace as you come before Me with a humble, repentant heart.

I have set you free, beloved! So you are free indeed (Jn 8:36)! Never again let the enemy deceive you into thinking you deserve condemnation (Col 2:8-10). Just stand in My love and in the completed work of the cross. Receive the victory that is yours, and walk as a conqueror in the shadow of My all-sufficient grace.

It's Not Too Late

There is therefore now no condemnation to those who are in Christ Jesus, who do not walk according to the flesh, but according to the Spirit.
Ro 8:1

*D*o not condemn yourself, My precious one, for your sins, shortcomings, and failures. Do not grieve that you have not done everything for Me that you could have, or even should have; for My mercies are fresh and new each day (La 3:22-23).

Consider the thief on the cross (Lk 23:39-43). Do you see that I used his life powerfully, even though there was nothing left he could do but humble himself and recognize Me as Lord? His life was all but over; he could not serve or witness. Yet, in My mercy, I used his last-minute conversion to witness to multitudes. His story says *it's never too late to be redeemed by My love.* Do you see that in My grace, love, and forgiveness, I transformed a wretched, sinful life into a powerful witness for all time—and all within the confines of the last few moments of his life?

So, My child, do not condemn yourself for time wasted. Simply know that I have the power to transform and to use all who humble themselves, no matter how late they receive Me, and no matter what sins they've committed (1 Jn 1:9). You see, in My mercy and grace, I transform ashes into beauty (Isa 61:3). I also cause *all* things to work for the good of those who love Me and are called according to My purposes (Ro 8:28). Beloved, I ask you, where's the expiration date on the promises in these verses? Where's the loophole for regret, guilt, or shame? Do you see there is nothing but pure grace, love, and hope within these verses?

Rejoice, beloved, and hold fast to the truth in these verses, for the truth will set you free (Jn 8:32)! Don't make an idol of your sins by focusing more on them than on My promise of forgiveness, love, and grace. Let Me be your perfection—the perfection of your past, present, and future (Heb 10:14). Do you see, My child? I make *all things* new, *all things* right (2 Co 5:17). So come unto Me, and let Me transform your life of ashes into beauty as I did with My humble, forgiven, blessed, and dearly loved thief.

You Are Completely Forgiven

As far as the east is from the west, so far has He removed our transgressions from us.
Ps 103:12
For He made Him who knew no sin to be sin for us, that we might become the righteousness of God in Him.
2 Co 5:21

My precious child, I want you to know deeper still the *complete* forgiveness that is yours in Christ. How often you have looked at yourself as filthy and abhorrent in My sight—unworthy and unable (so you thought) to enter into My presence. My beloved, this is a lie straight from the pit of hell. How I long for you to fully believe and receive the fact that, when I look at you, I see the purity and righteousness of Jesus (Eph 1:4).

Think upon this: You know that I am pure and holy, and that the filth of sin causes separation between Me and My creation (Isa 59:2). But, My love, Jesus became that sin for you. That's why He cried out in agony, "My God, My God, why have You forsaken Me?" (Mt 27:46). He suffered the agony of separation from Me, so you would never have to experience that separation (Eph 2:13). He took your filth, laid it upon Himself, and gave you His purity!

Beloved, how many times have you felt the sweetness of My presence? How many times have you reveled in My touch, voice, guidance, protection, provision, and so much more? My precious one, do you see that because sin causes separation from Me, your sins would have to be completely removed in order for Me to draw so near? Rejoice, My beloved, for whom My Son sets free is free indeed (Jn 8:36)! You are completely free from the stain of sin! Truly, you are holy and without blemish in My eyes. This has always been My plan, and My heart leaps for joy when My children know they are always welcome in My loving presence (Heb 4:16).

Since time began, My desire has been to walk with My children in the cool of the day (Ge 3:8). So, do not hide yourself any longer, My love, for you are fully adorned in the righteousness of Christ (2 Co 5:21). Walk with Me. Talk with Me. Dance with Me. Sing with Me. Abide in Me. Refuse, as Moses did, to move on without Me (Ex 33:15-16). Resist the devil's lie that you can't reside in My presence, and he will flee (Jas 4:7). Dwell with Me (Ps 91:1)—every day, every moment, every breath. Come unto Me, beloved. Receive My forgiveness, rest in My favor (Mt 11:28-30), and taste and see that I am good (Ps 34:8).

I Identify With You

Therefore, it was necessary for Jesus to be in every respect like us, His brothers and sisters, so that He could be our merciful and faithful High Priest before God. He then could offer a sacrifice that would take away the sins of the people. Since He Himself has gone through suffering and temptation, He is able to help us when we are being tempted.
Heb 2:17-18, NLT
Let us cling to Him and never stop trusting Him. This High Priest of ours understands our weaknesses, for He faced all the same temptations we do, yet He did not sin. So let us come boldly to the throne of our gracious God. There we will receive His mercy, and we will find grace to help us when we need it.
Heb 4:14-16, NLT
Therefore He is able, once and forever, to save everyone who comes to God through Him. He lives forever to plead with God on their behalf.
Heb 7:25, NLT

My beautiful child, I want you to know how deeply I relate to you and understand you (Ps 103:13-14). I want you to know that I fully understand how difficult life's circumstances can be: injustice, cruelty, misunderstanding, rejection, isolation, pain, and grief. I lived on this earth, and I experienced much pain. I suffered willingly and with great love for you. I experienced everyday life on earth just as you do now. I did this so you would realize that I not only died for you, but I also *lived* for you.

I lived every moment for you, according to My Father's will. In so doing, I fulfilled everything you are unable to fulfill (Ro 8:2-4). I suffered, and I was tempted in all the ways in which you suffer and are tempted. Yet, I did not sin. I continually remained in the center of My Father's will (Jn 5:19), determined to fulfill My purpose for walking upon the earth—I came to redeem you (Jn 3:16). And, in order to do so, I needed to fully identify with you. I needed to fully experience your suffering, temptations, and struggles. In the end, I also needed to take on your sin (2 Co 5:21). I did all this so I could overcome sin and death in your place, and then give you the power to overcome it through Me.

I want you to realize that because I so thoroughly identify with you, you can never suffer alone. I suffer with you (Mt 25:40). This means that when you are weak and struggling, I understand, I love you, and I'm interceding for you (Heb 7:25). When you are faltering and feel as if you will not be able to persevere, I understand, I love you, and I'm interceding for you. When you feel as if you have failed Me, I understand, I love you, and I'm interceding for you. For although I did not fail My Father, I did take on your sins, fully experiencing their impact and suffering the consequences. You see, My beloved, I really do understand.

So come boldly before My throne of grace. Commune with Me: internalize Me, so you may abide in Me and I in you (Jn 6:55-56). Do you see, My beloved, how the communion meal reflects the depth of identification I have with you? I lived for you, identifying with you to the point of literally becoming flesh and blood. I did this so that you could, in turn, identify with Me: I took on your sins, struggles, and temptations, so you could take on My righteousness (Ro 5:18-19).

So realize the wonder of the communion meal: the profound, intimate, communion and oneness we share, and the deep understanding and identification I have with you. Know that I live *in* you and identify *with* you as I live *for* you. In return, I want you to live in Me, taking on My likeness, while trusting that I intercede for you continually and love you with an unconditional, everlasting love.

Be Free

For if you forgive men their trespasses, your heavenly Father will also forgive you. But if you do not forgive men their trespasses, neither will your Father forgive your trespasses.
Mt 6:14-15

I want you to be completely free, My beloved, free from the bondage of *all* sin. This includes freedom from bondage that can result when others sin against you. Although, in reality, all sin is against Me and Me alone (Ps 51:4). Jesus stayed free from any bondage that could have oppressed Him when others sinned against Him. He modeled His freedom most profoundly the moment He said, "Father forgive them, for they know not what they do" (Lk 23:34), as the nails were being driven into His body.

Beloved, I want you to follow Jesus' example of living in freedom. In order to do this you need to realize that the freedom He enjoyed resulted from choosing to forgive. Can you see that My Son never internalized the impact of the sin being committed against Him? Can you see that He did not dwell for even a moment upon thoughts of resentment, judgment, criticism, hate, or vengeance? Do you see any hint of pride or self-righteousness in My Son even though He truly was righteous? Can you see that He did not look upon those sinning against Him through the eyes of their sin, but through the eyes of love and forgiveness (Jn 3:17)?

Jesus simply forgave immediately. He does this every day with you when you confess your sins (1 Jn 1:9). My love, and I want you to do the same for others (Lk 17:3-4). In fact, I command you to forgive, even as you have been forgiven (Mt 18:21-35).

Doesn't My forgiveness of your sin set you free from bondage (Jn 8:33-36) as you choose to repent and walk in that freedom (Ro 8:15-18)? Well, you also need to understand that when you obey Me in choosing to forgive others, the bondage of sin that is broken is within *you*—the one doing the forgiving (Mt 6:14-15).

My precious child, when you choose to forgive, you are living free from the bondage of other's sins against you that would otherwise be perpetuated and grow within *you*. How many times have you recited the sins of others against you in your mind and consequently felt more and more agitated, angry, critical, judgmental, unsettled, self-righteous, prideful, and even defiled? I'm telling you that the defilement is real, but the source of defilement is *not* the sins of the other: it's *your* sin of unforgiveness (Mk 11:25-26).

"But the fruit of the Spirit is love, joy, peace, longsuffering, kindness, goodness, faithfulness, gentleness, and self-control" (Gal 5:22). But how can you experience the gift of My fruits when you insist on hanging onto bitterness, resentment, judgment, hate, vengeance, and unforgiveness? I am calling you, My beloved, to take every thought, every inkling of bitterness and unforgiveness captive; for the weapon of forgiveness is mighty in defeating the kingdom of darkness (2 Co 10:3-5).

Remember, there is peace for those who keep their minds continually focused on Me (Isa 26:3); for when your mind is preoccupied with My unfathomable grace and love (Eph 2:4-6, 3:16-19), harboring unforgiveness becomes impossible. This is how My children overflow with My goodness, grace, love, forgiveness, and joy. This is how those who do not yet know Me will witness and experience My goodness, mercy, and love. This is what will inspire them to turn to Me and give Me glory (Mt 5:16).

So, I am calling you to forgive, My child, because I want you and others to experience the freedom that your willingness to forgive brings (Ro 6:22-23).

So be free, My beloved. Be free.

My Love Is Blind

You shall love your neighbor as yourself.
Mt 22:39

$\mathcal{B}$eloved, who is your neighbor? I know you have heard this many times, but I ask you again; who is your neighbor?

I want you to stop dividing where you were never meant to divide. Stop delineating in your mind between saint and sinner or between believer and unbeliever. I want you to start seeing that in this world there are only neighbors.

I want you to start seeing the world as flat, with everyone on the same level—no mountains, no valleys—no one is elevated above another, no one is less than another. As far as your love, receptivity, warmth, openness, and compassion for people is concerned, I want you to be blind to the delineation of godly versus ungodly: after all, isn't that what I did when I sacrificed My Son on the cross while *you* were yet My enemy (Ro 5:8-10)? My love knows no bounds.

Do you see, a bit more clearly, the wonder of My love—sending My one and only Son to save a world *that was at enmity* with Me? For while you were yet My enemy, I loved you to the point of sacrificing My Son (Jn 3:16): Jesus' arms were nailed wide open on the cross, mirroring My open arms that welcome *everyone* in a tender, loving embrace—whether they have turned to Me in love, or whether they are yet My enemy.

This is why I tell you to bless your enemies and to love those who hate you (Mt 5:43-45, Lk 6:27): I'm not asking you to do anything I haven't already done for you (Isa 53:3, 5, 12). This is why I tell you that you must forgive seventy times seven (Mt 18:21-22). This is why I tell you to love your neighbor as you love yourself. Remember, *all* people are your neighbors. And I am the Lord of all, whether or not those who do not believe understand that fact or not; I am their God, just as I am your God (Jer 32:27).

My heart is for all people; I lovingly created everyone. That makes Me everyone's Father—whether they realize it or not. I love everybody with the same extraordinary, inconceivable love that can never be diminished or taken away, no matter who they are or what they've done (Ro 8:38-39). I love everyone so much that I sent My Son to die, because all have sinned and fallen short of My glory (Ro 3:23-24, 1 Jn 1:10). Everyone includes you, My child, and it includes your neighbors who have not yet received what I have already done for them.

So, precious one, do not concern yourself with who is wheat and who is yet a tare (Mt 13:24-30). Remember, I tell the servant not to divide the wheat from the tares, but to leave that job to the reapers at the end of the harvest. So be blind in your love, My child—love both the wheat and the tares as I do. Let My grace flow through you to everyone: Be merciful as I am merciful (Lk 6:36). Be gentle as I am gentle (Mt 11:29). Be loving as I am loving (1 Jn 4:19).

Does this seem impossible to you? Remember, you are completely unable to do any of this without Me at your side (Jn 15:5). And rejoice, for My strength is made perfect in your weakness.

So ask, and you shall receive (Mt 7:7, 21:22). Ask for the same outrageous, extraordinary love that I have for all people. Fix your gaze upon Me, and be transformed more and more into My likeness (2 Co 3:18). Then shine your light for all to see, and captivate your neighbors with My love (Mt 5:14-16).

Love Begets Love

Love your enemies, bless those who curse you, do good to those who hate you, and pray for those who spitefully use you and persecute you.
Mt 5:44
Therefore you shall be perfect, just as your Father in heaven is perfect.
Mt 5:48

What has drawn you to My side but My great love for you? Do you not marvel at the fact that before you even knew or accepted Me—while you were yet following after your own lusts, desires, and ambitions—I loved you and even died for you (Ro 5:8)? Isn't this why you have given your heart to Me in love—because I first loved you (1 Jn 4:19)?

Do you see that love begets love—even in one's enemies? Love has the power to reproduce itself; I loved you while you were yet My enemy, and that begat love in you for Me (Ro 5:10-11). Do the same for your enemies, My beloved, and witness the miracle of love begetting itself.

So I say to you, be perfect in love as I am perfect; follow My example. When I was reviled, I did not revile in return. Instead, I humbly allowed Myself to be crucified so that everyone would have the opportunity to experience My healing love that restores a right relationship with Me (1 Pe 2:21-25). Notice the example of the submissive wife, who even though her husband does not obey My Word, lovingly remains by his side in the hope that some day he will follow Me (1 Pe 3:1-2).

So, My child, choose love rather than hate (Pr 10:12). Hate stirs up strife, dissension, chaos, fear, and all sorts of evil. But love covers a multitude of sin (1 Pe 4:8). Love has the potential to restore many to My side. Remember, I have commanded you to go and make disciples of all nations (Mt 28:19). Then go, My child, and capture those who are lost, with My love, just as I have captured you.

*The LORD your God
In your midst,
The Mighty One,
Will save.
He will rejoice over you
With gladness,
He will quiet you
With His love,
He will rejoice over you
With singing.*
Zephaniah 3:17

Savor Your Savior

Praise the Lord; praise God our savior! For each day He carries us in His arms. Our God is a God who saves! The Sovereign LORD rescues us from death.
Ps 68:19-20, NLT
Let Your salvation, O God, set me up on high. I will praise the name of God with a song, and will magnify Him with thanksgiving.
Ps 69:29b-30
Your lovingkindness is better than life.
Ps 63:3

Be still, My child, and ponder your Savior. Let these words sink deeply into your innermost being; you are saved. I say it again; *you are saved*! O that you would cease from your strivings and simply believe.

Slow down. Be still and know; be still and believe that I am God (Ps 46:10). Stop striving to be and to do good; stop striving to be Me. I want you to understand that no one is good—including you, My precious child—no one but Me (Mt 19:17). I actually want you to give up: I want you to cease from all striving. I want you to let go. I want you to realize your weakness, futility, inability, and brokenness (Ps 103:14-16, Ps 144:3-4). Then I want you to completely relax, trusting that My strength is made perfect in your weakness (2 Co 12:9). I want you to rest in what is already finished (Jn 17:2-4, 19:30): I want you to rejoice in all that your Savior has already accomplished for you. Savor Him, for this is faith; this is belief. That's right, My love, savor your Savior.

Look closely at Psalm 69:29b. My child, it does not say that it is *your* salvation that sets you on high. No, it is *My* salvation that sets you on high. Rejoice, beloved, for I have given you My salvation! There is no need for you to try to construct your own salvation; it's already done. Be still and know.

My salvation given to you is a gift of grace and love. It has absolutely nothing to do with what you have done, can do, or will do (Eph 2:4-9). It is simply a gift of love that reflects the essence of who I am—Love (1 Jn

4:16). All you need to do is believe (Jn 3:16). Then in your belief, I want you to submit and obey—not in an effort to save or perfect yourself, but as a reflection of your love and affection for Me (Jn 15:9-11). I want you to understand that your obedience is love, and only love; I have already given you My salvation. Remember, I do not require perfection from My children—no loving father would. I only require belief accompanied by love that is evidenced by obedience.

So when you find yourself stressed or striving to please Me, stop and believe; savor your Savior. When you feel overwhelmed, guilty, and burdened by your fallen, sinful state, stop and believe; savor your Savior. And when you are experiencing blessing and favor, stop and believe; savor your Savior. Rejoice, My child, all is well. Be still, and savor your Savior.

You Are My Reward

Greater love has no one than this, than to lay down one's life for his friends.
Jn 15:13

*M*y beloved, how I long for you to understand the depth of My love for you (Eph 3:17-19): I want you to know that you are well worth the suffering I endured on the cross. I would do it all over again if it would bring just one of My lost ones to My side. You see, My child, I knew you as I hung there (Jer 1:4, Ro 8:29); that's what kept Me there. I could have come down from the cross at any moment, sparing Myself agony and humiliation (Mt 26:52-54). However, the knowledge of you being My future bride kept Me there with great love and expectancy (Rev 19:7-9).

I want you to know that I do not look at you as the one who drove the nails into My hands and feet, even though it was for your sins that I laid down My life. No, My beloved, I see you as holy and without blame (Eph 1:4), My cherished reward (Ps 28:9, 33:12), My friend, and My bride—well worth the price of all I endured: this is the depth of My love for you (Jn 3:16).

So do not let Satan convince you that you are unwanted and unwelcome in My presence. Do not let him convince you that you are damaged and worthless and thus beyond the reach of My love (Ro 8:33, 38-39). Have I ever made anything that is worthless (Ge 1:31)? Would I have joyfully volunteered to suffer death on a cross for a reward that is worthless? How could you possibly be worthless? You bear My image (Ge 1:26)! Remember, long before I made the world, I chose you to be a part of My family (Eph 1:5), though I fully knew beforehand your every sin and shortcoming. Yet, the very thought of you living forever in My courts gives Me great pleasure.

Now do you understand how I delight in you—how I sing and dance for joy that you have received Me as your Love and your Lord (Isa 62:4b, 5b, Zep 3:17)? *You* are My inheritance (Heb 1:2)! *You* are worth the suffering I endured on the cross. And now I'm receiving My precious reward—*you*! Joy bursts through every cell in My body knowing that you are Mine both now and in eternity (Heb 12:2, Rev 21:3).

I Hold Out My Scepter For You

All the king's servants and the people of the king's provinces know that any man or woman who goes into the inner court to the king, who has not been called, he has but one law; put all to death, except the one to whom the king holds out the golden scepter, that he may live. Yet I myself [Esther] have not been called to go in to the king these thirty days.
Est 4:11
Now it happened on the third day that Esther put on her royal robes and stood in the inner court of the king's palace [uninvited], across from the king's house, while the king sat on his royal throne in the royal house, facing the entrance of the house. So it was, when the king saw Queen Esther standing in the court, that she found favor in his sight, and the king held out to Esther the golden scepter that was in his hand. Then Esther went near and touched the top of the scepter. And the king said to her, "What do you wish, Queen Esther? What is your request? It shall be given to you—up to half the kingdom!"
Est 5:1-3

My precious child, My bride, and My beloved, so many times you have hesitated to come before your King, fearing My wrath, condemnation, anger, rejection, or even subtle snubbing or mild irritation. You have been so aware of your sinful, fallen state, and you have been aware that My precious Son suffered for your sake. So many times you have come to Me with a burden on your back that you were *never* meant to carry. You've believed that because My Son suffered in your place, you are a burden to Me, and a source of pain, grief, irritation and inconvenience.

My beautiful one, do not forget about My scepter of love and grace, or about My delight in you as My bride (Isa 62:5b). Do not forget about the favor I give to you because you seek Me and My ways (Ps 5:12, Pr 8:35). Remember, it pleased Me to bruise My Son and put Him to grief (Isa 53:10). Why did it please Me? Because I love you so much that it gave Me great joy to ensure that, if you chose to return My love, you could live with Me for eternity (Jn 3:16).

My dear one, have you felt the sting of hurt when those around you made it clear to you that you were inconveniencing them? Have you been timid and hesitant at times to approach others because you know you had disappointed or hurt them? Have you been wounded by those who refused to offer you their scepter of love, grace, and favor? My beloved, you need to remember that I am not like others who sometimes give of themselves begrudgingly, hesitantly, sparingly, conditionally, and resentfully. Rather, I always give of Myself freely, willingly, and joyfully—even to the point of death on a cross (Heb 12:2).

I am your King who holds out My scepter and says, "My precious bride, what do you request? My kingdom is yours" (Mt 25:34, Lk 12:32). So, My beloved, rest in the favor of your King: Approach Me boldly, assured of My love and grace (Heb 4:16). Come near. Touch My scepter that is always stretched toward you, and receive My healing, saving, unconditional embrace.

Know that I did not hang on the cross begrudgingly. Know that I do not resent the many hardships I endured for you—not even the cross—for you are My bride who is always welcome to come before My throne of grace.

So come boldly into My presence. Pour your heart out to Me confessing your sins, brokenness, and failures. My response to you will *always* be forgiveness (1 Jn 1:9). Then, I will stretch My scepter toward you, beckoning you to come even closer, and I will gently whisper, "What is it, My beloved? Ask and it shall be given unto you" (Mt 7:7-8).

You Were Not Created To Serve Me

"Teacher, which is the great commandment in the law?" Jesus said to him, "You shall love the LORD your God with all your heart, with all your soul, and with all your mind. This is the first and great commandment."
Mt 22:36-38
Therefore love is the fulfillment of the law.
Ro 13:10

How I long for you, My precious child, to understand that I did not create you to serve Me. My heart grieves that so many of My children believe their primary purpose in life is to serve. This is a lie. For I have told you clearly what you are called to do: You are simply called to love Me. Hear My heart, My beloved; I just want you to love Me.

I created you out of great love, and I created you *for* love (Jer 31:3, Jn 15:9). I created you so I could express Myself; for I *am* love (1 Jn 4:8). My will for you is to walk in My love: I want you to receive My love then give it back to Me. I want you to abide in Me, dwell with Me, cherish Me, and delight in Me, as I cherish and delight in you (2 Th 3:5). I created you for a loving relationship with Me. That's why I tell you that loving Me is the most important commandment. That's why I tell you that love is the fulfillment of the law.

If I had created you to serve Me, I would have created you to be like a robot who would have been much more efficient and obedient to do My will. But no, I do not want mindless or obligatory service. And do I want your service in an effort to earn or prove anything: I just want your love.

I call you My friend (Jn 15:15), not My servant. I call you My child (Ps 82:6b), not My servant. I call you My bride (Isa 62:5b), not My servant. *You are My family.* So stop coming to Me as the prodigal son, ready to be My servant in an effort to express remorse over sin, or to live the way you think you should, or to live the way you think I want you to live. No, My precious child! I run to you, lovingly wrapping My arms around you, putting My signet ring upon your hand and *making you My heir* (Lk 15:17-24)!

I have adopted you into My family (Eph 1:5), enabling you to walk hand in hand with Me in a delightful, joy-filled, loving, and intimate relationship. However, it's impossible for you to realize the full extent of My love and grace for you if you insist on being My servant.

You must know My love first, then choose to serve out of love and delight in Me—never out of a sense of obligation or coercion. I never force or coerce. I only love: I reach out to you with open arms, longing for you to run into them and remain there forever. Then we can take action together, arm in arm, as a loving team, never making the act of service more important than our love for each other.

So look into your heart, My beloved. Why are you serving Me? Are you afraid? Driven? Obligated? Then stop. Realize that I love you, and that I created you for love. Nestle in My arms. Abide in Me. Then and only then can you serve out of love—the only right, good, and pure reason to serve.

Always remember that experiencing, expressing, and walking in My love is your primary purpose—never service. Then everything that is needed will flow out of your loving relationship with Me.

You Are My Friend

Abraham believed God, and it was accounted to him for righteousness. And he was called the friend of God.
Jas 2:23

My beloved friend, take a close look at the sequence of events in Abraham's life that brought about My friendship with him: James 2:23 is a quote from Genesis 15:6. Do you see that I called Abraham My friend well before he offered his son Isaac on the altar (Ge 22:9-10)? Do you see that I called him friend when all he did was believe he would become the father of many descendents (Ge 15:5-6), yet while he doubted he would inherit Canaan? He doubted whether he would receive the Promised Land in spite of the fact that I had just told him he would (Ge 15:7-8). Still, I called him "friend."

Take a closer look at Abraham's ability to believe My promise that he would have many descendants *through his aged wife Sarah* (Ge 16:1-3). Do you see that even in this matter his faith was not complete? Still, I called him "friend." Abraham heard and believed, but in a very limited way. His willingness to sleep with Hagar to try to produce the heir I promised him is evidence of his inability to fully believe. Still, I called him "friend."

This is the same man who lied to the Egyptians about Sarah's true identity because he was afraid for his life (Ge 12:11-13). He did this *after* I had promised him I would make him a father of a great nation (Ge 12:2). How could he have been afraid for his life when at that time he had no children, and I had promised him that he would be the father of many? Do you see how limited Abraham's faith really was? Do you also see the extent of My love and grace in calling him "friend"?

I don't tell you this so you can feel comfortable in your sins and shortcomings (Ro 6:1-2). Rather, I want you to understand that My friends are common people who struggle: My friends are those who are able to believe Me in certain areas of their lives, yet struggle with doubt in other areas. My friends are those who sometimes sin against Me, but who refuse to turn their backs on Me altogether.

As you look closely at Abraham's life, you will see a progression of faith. Before I called him out of Ur, he was a pagan (Jos 24:2). However, step by step, he came to know, understand, and follow Me more fully as he chose to invest and utilize the little bit of faith and understanding he had. *"But to those who use well what they are given, even more will be given. But from those who are unfaithful, even what little they have will be taken away"* (Lk 19:26, NLT). Gradually, he was transformed from a pagan, to a man who willingly offered his precious son to Me on an altar.

Beloved, do you see yourself in Abraham? Do you understand that I call *you* My friend—even in the midst of your incomplete faith and faltering steps? All I ask is that you use the little faith you have. In turn, I promise to build upon your faith as you act upon what you have been given. And rejoice, beloved, for in that process of growing and maturing, I will call you "friend."

*Trust in the LORD
With all your heart,
And lean not on your*
Proverbs 3:5

Judge Not

"The Lord knows the thoughts of the wise, that they are futile."
1 Co 3:20

*M*y beloved child, why do I tell you not to judge others? Because only I can accurately see into a person's heart: only I can know a person's true desires in spite of their struggles with sin (1 Sa 16:7).

Consider the laborers in the Master's vineyard: Each of them arrives at different times of the day. Yet, at the day's end, they receive the same wages (Mt 20:1-16). I want to take this parable a bit further with you so that you can understand just how unable you are to judge another human being based on what you see.

Consider two laborers: Matthew is a happy, healthy individual, who is married to a loving and supportive wife. Upon arising in the morning, his wife greets him lovingly and prepares breakfast for him before he leaves home to work in the vineyard. He drives to work and arrives promptly, ready to labor a full day in the vineyard. He is a good worker, and his efforts are highly visible and obvious as he brings in many grapes for the Master of the vineyard.

Peter is another laborer in the vineyard. He has struggled with poor health for many years, suffering with physical pain, weakness, and fatigue. He has no wife—no one to prepare breakfast for him, no one in the home to encourage him. He is poor. He has no car, and his shoes are worn through, providing him with little protection from the elements.

He physically struggles to get out of bed, but he's determined. He wants so badly to get to the vineyard so he can serve the Master he loves. He wills himself to rise in the morning. Then he walks ten miles to the vineyard, refusing to give in to his pain, weakness, and fatigue. He arrives one hour before the vineyard closes for the day. He is dirty and exhausted, and desperately needs to rest, so he asks the Master of the vineyard for permission to rest a bit before he begins his labors.

The Master, knowing everything Peter overcame to get to the vineyard, lovingly responds to him by putting His arm around him, offering him a drink and telling him to rest.

Meanwhile, Matthew sees Peter's tardiness and lack of production and becomes irate. He had arrived on time, worked all day under the hot sun, and produced much for the Master. He thinks to himself, "How dare Peter arrive here so late and so filthy? How dare he accept water from the Master and ask to rest when he has done absolutely nothing in the Master's vineyard?"

Do you see, My child, how Matthew just put a plank in his own eye by judging the speck in Peter's eye (Lk 6:41-42)? Do you see that My ways are not your ways, and that My thoughts are higher than your thoughts (Isa 55:8-9)? Do you see how it was a relatively simple thing for Matthew to work all day in My vineyard compared to all that Peter had to overcome? Do you see how Matthew's bare-bones minimum—arriving at the vineyard—was Peter's triumph?

I ask you, My precious child, when did each man's labor begin? I tell you that Matthew's labor began when he entered the vineyard. Peter's labor, however, began the moment he endeavored to rise out of bed.

So, My beloved, when you see others around you who are dirty, struggling, and seemingly not accomplishing much of anything for My kingdom, judge not. Remember, only I know the heart.

The Truth Shall Set You Free

"If you abide in My word, you are My disciples indeed. And you shall know the truth, and the truth shall make you free."
Jn 8:31-32

*B*eloved, I want you to ponder and receive these words I have for you, for they come from My heart:

I love you, My dear one (Jer 31:3, Jn 3:16, Ro 1:7). I delight in you (Isa 62:4b, 5b, Zep 3:17). You are the apple of My eye (Dt 32:10b). You have been born again into My kingdom (Jn 3:3), making you a new creation in Christ: The old things have passed away, behold, all things are new (2 Co 5:17). You are My royal heir (Gal 4:7, Eph 1:11). When I look at you, I see the righteousness of Christ (1 Co 1:30, 2 Co 5:21), for in His death and resurrection, you have inherited his purity and holiness (Eph 1:4-6).

Are you able to receive My words, My child? Are you able to walk in the light of these truths? Remember, there is nothing negative, condemning, or oppressive in Me (Ro 8:1, 33); I have come to save the world, not to condemn, or to judge it (Jn 3:17). And, since I have not yet returned a second time to judge the world, then I am still saving the world (Jn 12:47-48)! I am still setting the captives free (Isa 61:1, Lk 4:18, 21), and I am still offering life in abundance (Jn 10:10)! So, never again listen to a negative, fearful, condemning, or oppressive voice. Those voices go against all that I am and all that I have done for you.

Remember, however, that I chasten those I love (Rev 3:19). But, if there is no love or desire for your freedom in the "conviction," then you are listening to a voice other than My own. You also need to remember that there may be times when My convicting words are difficult for you to receive. But, when you do receive them, they will bring truth, light, freedom, and the opportunity to grow and become more like Me. Satan, on the other hand, uses shame, guilt, oppression, and fear in an effort to discourage and tear you down. Do you see the difference? How dare

Satan accuse and condemn you who are made in My own image (Ge 1:26-27)!

This also means that *you need to stop judging yourself so harshly.* And, you need to resist aligning yourself with the harsh judgments of others. For example, you and others may see yourself as a latecomer to My vineyard and judge harshly because you have not yet produced a big yield for Me (Mt 20:1-16). But beloved, I see your long and arduous trek to get to the vineyard: I see your determination to seek, love, and obey Me, in spite of everything the world has thrown at you. Do you see why I am so pleased with you? I want you to see yourself the way I see you, beloved. So stop judging yourself according to the way you, others, or Satan would judge (Ps 109:31, Isa 50:9).

Remember, your circumstances and sinfulness do not determine the way I see you; I see you through Christ's purity. I see the desires of your heart (Mt 5:8, Ac 15:8). A drug addict, for instance, may hate his behavior and may be fighting many, many demons and be losing in the flesh. But, his heart may be utterly consumed with a desire to get to know Me, follow Me, and walk in My light.

I see the heart, My child. When a person confesses and repents, I forgive them seventy times seven (Mt 18:21-22). I do not see the struggle they're in as far as judging them is concerned: I see their desire to win the battle. I see their desire to overcome.

There are many, however, whose minds and hearts do not truly desire Me: They have settled for religion and tradition as usual. Their own fleshly lusts have become their gods. They have no real interest in seeking or following Me. Rather, they desire to maintain their own comfortable lifestyles and to seek the praise and adoration of their fellow man (Mt 23:25-28, Lk 11:42-44). Do you see the true desire, or lack thereof, in their hearts as well?

They may be volunteering in the church, giving money to the poor, and attending Bible studies and seminars. Yet, all the while, they have no real interest in dying to self or following Me in any sincere way whatsoever. They have no spiritual battles, because they have joined the enemy. Consequently, the enemy can leave them alone—happy and complacent.

Beloved, if I am convicting you even now as you read, then repent. Seek to truly follow Me. Then I will rejoice and embrace you as My beloved prodigal who has returned home (Lk 15:11-24). I will show you the way, and you will be free indeed.

Meanwhile, the drug addict may appear to hate Me because of the battles he appears to be losing. However, his heart is set on Me: There is no complacency. He wants to die to self. He wants to follow Me. He's stumbling all over the place. *But*, he's on the path that leads to everlasting life, because his desires are sincerely set on Me (Ps 37:4-6).

Others can look very convincingly like they are on the right path. They often make their sacrifices to Me very visible while criticizing others for their lack of piety. Yet, in reality, they have no true desire to seek and obey Me.

Do you see why you must not judge anyone (Mt 7:1)? Do you see the futility of ever comparing your deeds and actions to those of another? Do you see why you must not look at the circumstances in anyone's life, in attempting to determine their heart for Me? Only I can know the heart, and *the heart is all that matters*.

Remember, in determining your standing with Me—your eternal destiny, and My delight and pleasure in you—the battle is irrelevant. Even how you're doing in the battle is irrelevant, as long as your heart's desire is to follow Me. Do you understand?

This is true because when I look at you, I see My Son's righteousness; you are holy and blameless in My sight because I have removed your sins as far from you as the east is from the west (Ps 103:12). My grace is sufficient for your every sin, every stumble, every shortcoming, every failure, and even every success (2 Co 12:9).

When your heart desires Me and My ways, in spite of the sins with which you may be struggling, you are a new creation and My royal heir. That's the way I see you: You're the apple of My eye. My love for you is without limit, without condition, and without wavering. My delight in you is constant; I even delight in you as you stumble. But I do not delight in the stumble itself. That's the difference between seeing your heart, versus focusing on your sins.

You have been set free from the bondage of sin and death (Ro 6:18, 23). That means you are free from sin's power to condemn you. Because of the blood of Christ, I no longer associate you with sin. This is what it means to be free indeed.

You are free indeed! Won't you rejoice and walk in that freedom, ceasing to see yourself through the lens of your sin—a lens that, when you desire Me and all that I have for you, doesn't even exist anymore? Do not let Satan convince you that that lens still exists. He is a liar (Jn 8:44), but I am the truth (Jn 14:6). And the truth shall set you free!

In Whom Do You Confide?

Love covers a multitude of sin.
1 Pt 4:8
God is love.
1 Jn 4:8

My beloved, where do you go when you're feeling particularly vile and unacceptable? Do you go inward, condemning yourself for the way you're feeling or behaving (Ro 8:1)? Do you keep the secret of your struggles to yourself? Or, do you go to a trusted friend in whom you can confide? Maybe it's a pet that hears and knows your darkest side. Or do you immerse yourself in a hobby in order to creatively express that which you dare not express in any other way? Whom do you trust to understand and accept you in ways that no one else can?

My precious one, I know you feel safe confiding and expressing yourself in these ways—to these people, and through these things. But I want you to know that *I am safer still.*

Yes, I have commanded you to confess your sins one to another that you may experience healing (Jas 5:16). However, you need to know that, as safe as you feel confiding in and expressing yourself to whomever or whatever it is you have chosen, I am even safer.

How I long for you to run into My arms knowing that you are welcome in this—the safest and best place—to receive understanding, peace, joy, forgiveness, mercy, and unconditional love. Remember, I know everything there is to know about you (Ps 139:1-4, Heb 4:13): I know your deepest, darkest side—your struggles, weaknesses, sins, and nebulous thoughts and feelings. Yet, I love you with an everlasting love (Jer 31:3, Ro 8:38-39). *The power of My love overcomes the power of your sin every single time* (Pr 10:12b, 1 Pe 4:8)! It's not even a close fight.

So come to Me, My beloved. Confide in Me. Experience My loving arms around you as you tell Me everything. Know the joy of receiving My unconditional love in the very midst of the shadows in your life:

This is faith. This is trusting and believing in the finished work of the cross. This is My desire. This is My love for you.

Abide In My Love

As the Father loved Me, I also have loved you; abide in My love. If you keep My commandments, you will abide in My love, just as I have kept My Father's commandments and abide in His love. These things I have spoken to you, that My joy may remain in you, and that your joy may be full.
Jn 15:9-11

How I long for you to abide in Me and Me in you. All that is required is that you obey My commandments, which are given to you in tender love, that you may avoid the pain and heartache of living outside My will (Dt 11:26-28). Follow Me with love in your heart; obey My commandments, and you shall know joy.

You must know, dear one, that there is no need for striving or fear when seeking to follow and obey Me. You can simply rest in Me and My love (Ps 46:10, Isa 30:15).

Let Me show you two very different scenarios: In the first example, My precious child is busy scrambling around the house cleaning and preparing. Every once in awhile, she glances over her shoulder at Me, while I stand patiently waiting. She is hoping that I will see how much she loves Me as evidenced by all the hard work she is doing. It is as if she were saying to Me, "Look at everything I am doing for You. I hope You are pleased with all my efforts. I want to serve You continually, because I want to prove my love for You. Are You feeling my love? Do You see how much I love You?"

Now let's look at another scenario: I walk through the front door of My child's home, and she immediately runs into My arms, telling Me how much she loves Me. Then we converse back and forth, thoroughly enjoying one another's company.

Which of these two scenarios do you believe touches Me more? Can you see how the first scenario is actually painful to Me? There's My precious child, running around the house, looking over her shoulder, desperately hoping in anxious anticipation that I will be pleased with her because of what she's done for Me. Can you see that, rather than love, she is actually revealing her fear of Me in her attempts to appease Me? Can you understand why I would *so be longing* for her to understand that I am *not* like that—that I do not take pleasure in efforts of appeasement or in efforts of proving one's self (Ps 51:16, Eph 2:8-9)? How sad I am when My beloved children do not know this about Me, and when they do not see Me for who I really am.

How would you feel, My beloved, if a child of yours frantically tried to do everything right in an effort to appease you and win your love, when you simply loved her all along? How would you feel if, when you walked in the door, instead of running into your arms, your child frantically tried to serve you in an effort to prove her love? Would it not hurt you to experience this? This is how I feel when you try to prove your love to Me. Attempting to prove your love to Me by frantically doing good works is really an effort to quell fears that you will experience My rejection and wrath if you don't prove yourself. Remember, My child, I loved you long before I even created the world—long before you were able to do anything at all (Eph 1:4). *It's not about what you do. It's about who I am.*

So run into My arms. It's exactly where I long for you to be. O, that you knew My desire for this one thing—that you would abide in My love for you. This is My desire (Mk 12:30). Then, all things become possible through Me, because you are no longer relying on your own efforts (Jn 15:5). Instead, you are trusting in My goodness and grace, and allowing Me to work through you. That is when I can make My will known to you (Jn 15:15). Once you realize who I am, and the free gift of grace I offer (Ro 3:27-28), you will be able to fully give yourself to Me and understand My plans for your life (Jer 29:11).

It is this complete surrender that unleashes My power and fruits of the Spirit to degrees beyond your wildest imagination. This is what Paul expressed when he said, "And I pray that Christ will be more and more at home in your hearts as you trust in Him. May your roots go down deep into the soil of God's marvelous love. And may you have the power to understand, as all God's people should, how wide, how long, how high, and how deep His love really is. May you experience the love of Christ, though it is so great you will never fully understand it. *Then* (emphasis mine) you will be filled with the fullness of life and power that comes from God. Now glory to God! By His mighty power at work within us, He is able to accomplish infinitely more than we would ever dare to ask or hope" (Eph 3:17-20, NLT).

You also must remember that My desire to have you in My arms *never* changes with any of your failures or sins: You don't need to appease Me. You don't need to make up for any of your shortcomings or sins. I am not that kind of a God. I don't take pleasure in sacrifices of guilt or in efforts to make up for your sin. I delight only in you in My arms (Mk 10:13-16).

Imagine yourself caring for a child, and you see him doing something naughty. As you stand there, he approaches you with a look of sincere regret for his behavior. Then, he reaches up to you, wanting you to pick him up and hold him so that he can whisper into your ear how sorry he is for misbehaving. Tell Me, would you reject his request to be held and comforted while he wraps his arms around your neck, telling you that he is sincerely sorry for being naughty?

How much more do I look upon My precious children, willing and longing to hold them while they confess their sins in My ear! This does not mean that I take sin lightly or that I do not discipline those whom I love (Heb 12:5-6, Rev 3:19). However, when you confess your sin, in My grace, I not only allow you to stay in My embrace while I discipline you, but I *long* for you to stay there (Ez 11:16): remember, nothing, not even My discipline, can snatch you out of My hand (Jn 10:28-29).

How would you feel if that same child, instead of reaching up to you and confessing his misdeed, fell at your feet and began hitting himself over and over, crying out to you in emotional distress, asking you to forgive him? What does this child's behavior say about who he thinks *you* are? Wouldn't this disturbing behavior tear at your heart? Wouldn't you long for him to know that you are not a beast who accuses and condemns (Rev 12:10), but a loving parent who forgives sincere hearts freely? Who dares accuse My children whom I have chosen for My own? I have given them right standing with Myself (Ro 8:33).

You see, My love, it is a lie that you must flog yourself emotionally, spiritually, or in any other way for the sins you have committed. It is a lie that you must do more than confess your sins from a sincere heart. Your confession gives you immediate right standing with Me, because of what Christ did for you on the cross.

Frequently, parents will change from suits and ties into their blue jeans before romping around with their young children, especially when they know that things are likely to get messy. Then, when the children reach up to be held with their runny noses and dirty little hands, the parent does not hesitate to pick them up. Isn't this what Jesus has done for all humanity? He set aside His deity and glory—took off His suit and tie—and He put on your sins (Jn 1:14). Now, He calls you to Himself saying, "Let the little children come to Me, and do not forbid them; for of such is the kingdom of God. Assuredly, I say to you, whoever does not receive the kingdom of God as a little child will by no means enter it" (Lk 18:16).

So come to Me, My child—runny nose and all—and I will scoop you up into My loving embrace. This is what it means to be free from the bondage of sin and death (Ro 8:1-2). For, in Christ, sin and death no longer have any power over your ability to rest secure in My arms forever. "Let the beloved of the Lord rest secure in Him, for He shields him all day long. And the one the Lord loves rests between His shoulders" (Dt 33:12, NIV).

"There is therefore *now*"—you don't have to wait until later—"no condemnation to those who are in Christ Jesus, who do not walk according to the flesh, but according to the Spirit" (Ro 8:1). Do you see that "walking according to the flesh" is not only referring to your behavior, but also to your identity? This means that you are not to identify yourself with your flesh. The flesh says, "You are struggling. You don't measure up. You are not good enough. You still have sin in your life. You can't experience God's loving embrace until you straighten yourself out." Instead, you are to walk according to the identity of the Spirit who says, "You are holy and righteous in My sight (Eph 1:4-5). There is nothing you can do to separate yourself from My love (Ro 8:38-39). I have crowned you with glory and honor" (Ps 8:5).

So run into My arms, My child. Confess what you need to confess. Know that I am holding you close. In My arms, My Spirit will nurture you, strengthen you, and set you free from the bondage of sin that would try to convince you that you don't belong in My embrace. My Spirit will also gently convict you, showing you the areas in your life that are in need of My healing love and in need of your willingness to let go and repent.

Within My embrace you will learn to run and leap upon the mountains as I say, "Arise, My darling, My beautiful one, and come with Me" (SS 2:10, NIV); serve Me, shining your light in this darkened world. Within My embrace you will also learn to continually rest in My love and in My favor no matter what you are doing: This is My love for you. This is who I am. This is the relationship for which you were created. This is My loving embrace that I long for you to receive and walk in all the days of your life. This is the victory over sin and death, now and for all eternity, through your precious Savior Jesus Christ.

*"I will never
Leave you
Nor forsake you."*
Hebrews 13:5

Right Here, Right Now

"And lo, I am with you always, even to the end of the age."
Mt 28:20

*P*onder this: I am with you—right here, right now. Just think, I, the Creator of the universe, Love personified (1 Jn 4:8), the all-powerful, all-knowing, merciful, good, gracious, humble, and gentle Lord am with you this very moment—and I love you with an unceasing love (Jer 31:3, Ro 8:38-39).

I am with you continually, beloved, so there is no reason to fear, worry, or strive. Hear Me, My precious one; I am with you, right here, right now. So let go of all your fears and rest in the knowledge that I am by your side, and I am *on* your side (Ro 8:31).

You may be experiencing illness, but I am right here, right now. You may be experiencing persecution, but I am right here, right now. You may be struggling financially, but I am right here, right now. You may be feeling hopeless within your marriage or family, but I am right here, right now. Remember, your current circumstances are transient, but I am eternal; I will *always* be with you (2 Co 4:16-18).

Cast all your cares upon Me, My beloved, because I am right here, right now (1 Pe 5:7). Be anxious for nothing. Instead, draw near to Me in prayer with thanksgiving, and I will give you peace (Php 4:6-7). Know that My loving, abiding presence will comfort and calm you in the midst of your trials as you focus on Me (Isa 26:3-4): I am your strength, your deliverer, and your refuge (Ps 18:1-3).

This is the secret the apostle Paul knew so well. This is why he was able to be content in all things (Php 4:11-12): He simply remained in Me, and I became his strength in the midst of his trials (Php 4:13). He understood and lived the truth that I am right here, right now.

So rest in Me, My beloved—right here, right now. For no matter what your life brings, My presence and My strength are greater still. Remember, I am with you in all things (Heb 13:5), supplying everything you need—right here, right now.

Who Are You Believing?

Every word of God proves true.
Pr 30:5, NLT
The LORD is faithful in all He says.
Ps 145:13, NLT
He is the one who keeps every promise forever.
Ps 146:6, NLT
Oh, the joys of those who trust the LORD....
Ps 40:4, NLT

*M*y precious one, I want you to be so much more aware of who you are believing in your moment-by-moment living. So many of My children are unaware that they are choosing to believe Satan, the father of lies (Jn 8:44), rather than My Holy Word (Ps 18:30).

Do you realize, My child, that when you entertain fear and doubt, you are believing the father of lies? I do not tell you this to shame you. Rather, I tell you this in a spirit of love that longs to set you free from the bondage of disbelief. I long to root you in a deep, unshakable faith, grounded in the knowledge that My Word is true. I long to expose the enemy's tactics that subtly attempt to cause My children to doubt Me.

Doubt was the very first tactic Satan used on My children in the Garden of Eden (Ge 3:1), and he is still up to his very old tricks: "Did God *really* say ...? Can you *really* believe Him? I don't think you can. Listen to me. I'll tell you the way things *really* are" (Gen 3:2-5). Do you see that Satan is trying to deceive My children all the way from Genesis through Revelation (Rev 12:9)? But rejoice, My child, for My Word possesses power and authority over Satan and all his ways (Lk 4:33-36).

Listen, beloved, to how I want you to apply this teaching: I want you to be aware and honest with Me, and with yourself, about the degree of doubt you may be experiencing. Remember, the truth will set you free (Jn 8:32). However, denial, or pretending that you believe, when in fact you are struggling, will only hinder you. So, for example, when you read in Psalm 23, "The LORD is my shepherd; I have everything I need"

(Ps 23:1, NLT), ask yourself if you honestly believe that verse. Realize that *I* am the One who is telling you that you *really do* have everything you need. Realize as well that Satan is the one who is saying, "The LORD really isn't your shepherd. You can't trust Him. You certainly do not have everything you need." Do you see that Satan will try to convince you that the opposite of what I say is true?

Whenever you find yourself not fully believing My Word, stop. Remember that, in that moment, you are believing the father of lies rather than your Lord who is the Way, the *Truth*, and the Life (Jn 14:6). Determine to believe Me. Turn to Me, and ask Me for help in your unbelief (Mk 9:24).

Look within, My beloved. Do not be afraid of what you will find; I already know what is there, and I love you (Heb 4:12-13). Confess your unbelief (1 Jn 1:9). Ask for a deep, unshakable faith in Me and My Word, and I will surely answer your prayer (Mt 7:7-11). Determine to no longer let Satan rob you of the fact that My Word is absolutely true (Ps 18:30, 33:4). Do not allow him to influence you to add or subtract from My Word through doubt or disbelief (Dt 4:2, Rev 22:18-19). Instead, be transformed by the renewing of your mind to believe Me rather than Satan (Ro 12:2). Know that I am faithful in all I say (Dt 7:9, 1 Co 1:9, Rev 19:11). And experience the unsurpassable peace of one who believes Me and My promises (Isa 26:3).

*I Am Trustworthy,
Even In Your Affliction*

And we know that all things work together for good to those who love God, to those who are called according to His purpose. For whom He foreknew, He also predestined to be conformed to the image of His Son, that He might be the firstborn among many brethren. Moreover whom He predestined, these He also called; whom He called, these He also justified; and whom He justified, these He also glorified.
Ro 8:28-30

My precious child, I want to talk to you about trusting Me in the presence of illness; I want you to know there can be many reasons an illness remains unhealed. Satan, however, would love to oppress you with his lie that, because you are ill, you are condemned, unloved, unworthy, and unwelcome in My arms. Beloved, do not let him torment you with the lie that if you only had enough faith, you would be healed. Do you see that he is trying to get you to have faith in your own faith, rather than faith in Me and My goodness? Remember, I have called you to have faith and trust in *Me*, not faith in faith.

My child, I want you to know, that you know, *that you know*, that nothing can separate you from My love (Ro 8:38-39), including infirmity. I want you to remember that whatever I allow in your life will be used for your good as you trust in Me and seek to walk in My purposes. In some cases, I cause good to come from an illness as My beloved child decides to draw nearer to Me, to seek harder after Me, to ask difficult questions, and learns to trust and lean on Me through the trial of being ill. Can you see that when this happens, My ill child is actually growing in his faith in spite of sickness? Never assume of yourself, or anyone else, that illness automatically reflects a lack of faith. Little do you know that My precious, struggling child could very well be growing in his faith as he learns to draw near to Me for strength and support.

I will use whatever it takes to encourage My loved ones to draw near, to stay near, and to grow in intimacy and maturity in their walk with

Me. For the rebellious Israelites of old, I used captivity to draw their attention and devotion back to Me. For some I use illness. For others I use different trials, each suited to speak to the individual. The ultimate reason behind all that I do and allow is to draw My loved ones to My breast (Mt 23:37).

Remember the blind man I healed, whose affliction was not caused by sin and rebellion (Jn 9:1-3)? Look closely at these verses, beloved. Notice how I draw attention away from My disciple's propensity to blame and toward My own goodness and glory.

Consider the godly remnant, the likes of Daniel, Habbakuk, Jeremiah and Nehemiah. They abided in Me and kept My commandments. Yet they suffered captivity along with those who were wicked and godless. You see, sometimes My obedient ones suffer because of the evil around them, not because they themselves have sinned (1 Pt 4:12-14). I tell you this so that you will not allow Satan to torment you with oppressive lies. Do not let him convince you that you must have done something to deserve to suffer, or that you do not have enough faith to be healed.

Remember, I heal those who do not yet believe as well as those who have faith in Me. So beware, My love, of completely erroneous conclusions made by people with good intentions. Job's friends, for example, were godly. Yet they came to completely inaccurate conclusions about Job and his relationship with Me when they sought to interpret the meaning of his afflictions (Job 8:6). This still happens today when people assume that there must be sin or a lack of faith behind all suffering and illness.

"By His stripes you are healed" (1 Pt 2:24). Do you see that the context in which this verse is found teaches that Jesus' suffering is what heals you from sin and frees you to live for what is right? Do you see that this verse is in the middle of several verses that teach you to endure unfair treatment with patience, as Jesus did, with the hope that others will be won over to Me because of your godly behavior (1 Pt 2:18-3:2)?

Do not let Satan torment you with the lie that, because of the stripes Jesus endured, everyone will automatically be physically healed. Consequently, there must be something spiritually wrong if you're struggling with illness. I *do* still heal miraculously. But that doesn't automatically mean that those who struggle with illness don't have enough faith to be healed: Sometimes I allow, in My wisdom, what I could easily heal with My power. I know the plans I have for you, My precious child, plans that are good, bring peace, hope, and a bright future (Jer 29:11). However, there are times when I ask you to be patient and to trust Me while in the midst of affliction.

Remember, what matters is My heart for you and your heart for Me. What matters is knowing that I love everyone so deeply that I gave My only Son to suffer and die, so that all who would believe—whether healthy, sick, slave, free, male, female, young, or old—would not die, but have eternal life (Jn 3:16, Gal 3:26-29).

So lift up your head, beloved, and give thanks in all things, for I am indeed good and trustworthy (1 Th 5:18). Receive My abundant love for you, and choose to walk with Me in trust, regardless of your circumstances. I promise that, no matter what difficulties you are experiencing, My goodness and mercy will follow you all the days of your life (Ps 23:6).

Let Me Be Your Relief

For I have learned in whatever state I am, to be content: I know how to be abased, and I know how to abound. Everywhere and in all things I have learned both to be full and to be hungry, both to abound and to suffer need. I can do all things through Christ who strengthens me.
Php 4:11-13

My dear one, are you uneasy, restless, angry, agitated, grieving, stressed, anxious or fearful? Then let Me be your relief. Focus your thoughts on Me, rather than on your difficult feelings and circumstances, and you will find relief—even in the midst of your difficulties. Remember, I am the light that shines round about you (Jn 8:12). To Me, the light and the darkness are both alike (Ps 139:11-12). Beloved, you need not fear any darkness when you are bathed in My light and under My care; I am the One who will ultimately deliver you from all darkness (Ps 18:28, 2 Ti 4:18).

Look to Me, beloved. I am your strength (Ps 62: 5-7). All that is good in your life comes from Me (Ps 85:12, Jas 1:17): I am the One who promises to cause everything to work for your good, because you love Me, and because I have called you according to My purposes (Ro 8:28). I am the Rock of your salvation (Ps 62:2). I am your Comforter (Isa 51:12, 2 Co 1:3-4). I am your Provider (Lk 12:22-28). And I am your heavenly Father who holds you in the palm of My hand (Ps 37:23-24).

So, receive My peace and My relief, beloved, even in the midst of troubling feelings and circumstances. This is the secret that Paul learned: He endured much hardship—infirmities, distress, persecution, the reproach of men, and a thorn in the flesh. Yet he learned to be content no matter what was happening to him or around him (2 Co 12:7-10).

Paul's secret was Me. He knew to look to Me for peace (Ps 29:11, Isa 26:3), relief, and strength (Ps 18:1, 32). My goodness, promises, and salvation, were more real to him than any transient earthly experience. That is how he could sing praises while imprisoned, in pain, and uncertain as to whether he would be executed for his faith (Ac 16:22-26): He kept proper perspective—an eternal perspective. He understood that his trials on earth were a mere blink of an eye (Mt 5:11-12) when compared to the joy of living with Me for eternity (Rev 21:1-7).

So, My beloved, look to Me for relief. Remember that every difficulty you experience is temporary. Know that as you determine to persevere and overcome, you will know great and eternal joy (1 Co 2:9, 2 Co 4:16-18). Draw near to Me in your troubles, and I promise I will draw near to you (Jas 4:8). I promise I will never leave you alone to deal with life's difficulties (Heb 13:5-6); I love you too much to ever turn My back on you. I love you with an eternal and everlasting love (Jer 31:3)—a love so great that I sent My beloved Son to die in your place (Jn 3:16, 15:13).

So, let Me be your relief, My precious one. Keep your gaze steadily fixed on Me, and I promise that I will personally wipe every tear from your eye.

The Whole Picture

And He said to me, "My grace is sufficient for you, for My strength is made perfect in weakness." Therefore most gladly I will rather boast in my infirmities, that the power of Christ may rest upon me. Therefore I take pleasure in infirmities, in reproaches, in needs, in persecutions, in distresses, for Christ's sake. For when I am weak, then I am strong.
2 Co 12:9-10

*M*y precious child, I want you to take your eyes off your weaknesses, and instead, trust in My strength and ability. Remember, *it's not about you.* It's not about what you are able to accomplish; it's not about you striving to make sure My purposes are fulfilled on earth. It's about Me; it's about what I want to accomplish through you as you yield to Me, and as you trust that My power is sufficient in your weakness.

Rejoice My child, for My grace and My strength really are sufficient for your every need and your every circumstance (Php 4:13). It's not about what you can do; it's about who I am and what I have planned for you (Jer 29:11, (Eph 1:18); it's about what My power can accomplish in and through your life (Eph 3:20).

I'm asking you to trust Me (Pr 3:5-6). And I'm asking you to stop looking at the weaknesses, hindrances, and barriers in your life. Instead, I want you to keep your eyes on Me, trusting in My ability and power in every situation (2 Co 3:4-5).

Look at Moses and the Israelites: They were pinned between the Red Sea and the advancing Egyptian chariots (Ex 14:10-12). They were weak. They were afraid. They were helpless. Obstacles surrounded them on every side, but that was *not* the whole picture.

The whole picture was that I was with the Israelites, loving, guiding, protecting, and providing for them. And, although I was hidden and invisible at the time, I was about to manifest My power and presence in an astonishing way (Ex 14:13-14, 21-30). Let this be a reminder to you, My child, that *your assessment of any situation is incomplete when you forget to consider My presence and power.*

Look at your own life. How many times have you been sure of a negative outcome only to be surprised when unforeseen doors suddenly opened wide? How many times have you been aware of My protection and provision as you narrowly escaped harm? Surely I tell you, there have been even more times when I fiercely protected you, and you were completely unaware! Can you see that My strength is indeed made perfect in your weakness?

So, what do you have to fear (Isa 41:13)? Do you see that your assessment of any situation is irrelevant when you fail to consider the whole picture? You are walking with the Most High God, and *My presence and power in your life changes everything* (Ps 28:7-8, 46:1)!

This does not mean that you will not experience hardship, trials, and suffering; even My Son experienced suffering while walking in the fullness of My power and presence. Remember, however, My power, protection, and provision brought Him triumphantly through His suffering; that same power now has Him seated at My right hand, far above all powers and principalities (Eph 1:19-22).

So, take your eyes off the obstacles in your life, My love, and rejoice. As you walk with Me, I will fulfill everything I have planned for you using your weaknesses to demonstrate My strength.

I am on your side (Ro 8:31-32, 37), My love, and *that* is the whole picture.

*The name of the LORD
Is a strong tower;
The righteous run to it
And are safe.*
  Proverbs 18:10

What Can Possibly Harm You?

"And I say to you, My friends, do not be afraid of those who kill the body, and after that have no more that they can do. But I will show you whom you should fear: Fear Him who, after He has killed, has power to cast into hell; yes, I say to you, fear Him! Are not five sparrows sold for two copper coins? And not one of them is forgotten before God. But the very hairs of your head are all numbered. Do not fear therefore; you are of more value than many sparrows."
Lk 12:4-7

Beloved, in this world you will have trials and troubles, but do not fear, for I have overcome the world (Jn 16:33). When you are struggling, feeling like you are surrounded by difficulties at every turn, or experiencing rejection by others because of your love for Me, rejoice, for I will personally wipe away your every tear (Rev 7:17). So, do not fear or despair, My precious one; I am the Lord who strengthens, helps, and upholds you in the palm of My hand (Isa 41:10). Sickness, death, darkness, pain, and suffering do not have the last say—I do! I am the One who has conquered the power of sin and death for all time (2 Ti 1:10).

You may be hard-pressed on every side, but you are not crushed. You may be perplexed, but, as you remain in Me, you will not give up in despair. You may be hunted and knocked down, but I will never leave you or forsake you (2 Co 4:8-10, Heb 13:5b). You are My beloved. I love you, and the very powers of hell will never be able to snatch you from Me (Jn 10:27-29).

Satan may try to take your health, possessions, family, friends, and even your life. But he cannot steal your eternity with Me (Rev 2:10-11)! So fight the good fight of faith. Do not surrender your heavenly destiny to the enemy (1 Ti 6:12). Remember, you are called to overcome, holding tightly to My promises (Heb 3:14). Remember, I, too, suffered and was tempted in all things. Yet I did not give in (Heb 4:14-16). So, you see My child, I am your compassionate Savior who knows your trials and who is well qualified to give you grace and help in your time of need.

So remain in Me, My beloved, and do not lose heart. Know that I am renewing your inner being daily even in the midst of great trials. Remember that your difficulties are only temporary, and that your faith and steadfastness during these times will bring you a great and everlasting reward (2 Co 4:16-18).

Rejoice, My child, for I am with you always (Mt 28:20), and I am your strength to overcome (Php 4:13).

Press On

Therefore we do not lose heart. Even though our outward man is perishing, yet the inward man is being renewed day by day. For our light affliction, which is but for a moment, is working for us a far more exceeding and eternal weight of glory.
2 Co 4:16-17

Take heart, My child, when you are persecuted, rejected, ridiculed, criticized, judged, misunderstood, and even faced with death because of your faith, for your eternal reward in heaven is great (Mt 5:11-12)! Know that, no mater what trials you are experiencing, I am by your side: I am your strength (Php 4:13). I am your light (Jn 8:12). And My glory shines through you as you persevere in Me.

Bearing My light (1 Th 5:5), however, can attract persecution, because the darkness hates the light and will do everything it can to snuff it out (Jn 15:18-20). However, I promise that My light shining through you will pierce that darkness (Jn 1:4-5, Col 1:12-13)! Remember, the Holy Spirit is living within you. He is the Spirit of Christ, the Word made flesh. And I promise that My Word living in you will not return void; it will prosper wherever I send you (Isa 55:11).

So, press on (Php 3:14), My beloved. Know that My presence within you as you persevere is accomplishing much more than you realize (Eph 3:20). Know that you are sealed and can never be taken from My hand as long as you determine to follow Me (Eph 1:13-14). You are My precious bride, and what I have joined together let no one put asunder (Mk 10:9). Rejoice, My beloved, for your reward in heaven is great. Greater still is My power and love at work within you—even now—even in the midst of trials and persecutions (1 Pe 4:12-14).

Know Who You Are

That the God of our Lord Jesus Christ, the Father of glory, may give to you the spirit of wisdom and revelation in the knowledge of Him, the eyes of your understanding being enlightened; that you may know what is the hope of His calling, what are the riches of the glory of His inheritance in the saints, and what is the exceeding greatness of His power toward us who believe, according to the working of His mighty power which He worked in Christ when He raised Him from the dead and seated Him at His right hand in the heavenly places, far above all principality and power and might and dominion, and every name that is named, not only in this age but also in that which is to come.
Eph 1:17-21

Do you see who you are, My precious child? Do you see the power that is at your disposal through Me? There is exceeding great power for those who believe! You no longer need to be intimidated by the powers of darkness that make their home on this earth. You are no longer of this world; you are a partaker of Christ and the kingdom of heaven (Heb 3:14)! You are My royal child, a co-heir with Christ. You sit with Me with all the powers of hell beneath your feet (Eph 2:6, Ro 8:16-17)! This power is yours today, yours now. For the kingdom of God is at hand. And My kingdom is the very source of power that heals the sick, raises the dead, and casts out demons (Mt 10:7-8).

Do not let darkness and difficulties distract you from the truth that you are My royal bride who abides and reigns with Me. You belong to the all-powerful Creator of the universe. I am always with you, so there is no reason to fear (Ps 23:4). Consider what happened to Peter when he took his eyes off Me and became intimidated by the fierceness of the waves beneath his feet (Mt 14:28-31). He began to sink. He doubted and feared because he focused on the threat of the waves around him rather than focusing on My promises and power.

So, be strong in Me, My child—built up, rooted, and firmly established in your faith. Know who and whose you are. Know that you sit and reign with Me far above any power or darkness. Do not let anything rob you of your understanding, or of your use of your rank and position in Me. Instead, remain confident that you are made complete in Me, the head of all principality and power (Col 2:6-10).

Let Me Be Your Portion

Whom have I in heaven but You? And there is none upon earth that I desire besides You. My flesh and my heart fail; But God is the strength of my heart and my portion forever.
Ps 73:25-26

Do not lose heart, My child, for I know your trials, difficulties, sorrows, and afflictions. Even in the midst of these I am continually with you, holding you in My powerful and protective grasp (Ps 73:23-24).

Beloved, do not give in to the temptation to stop living for Me because living a godly life seems too costly. When you see the lives of the ungodly all around you, how so many prosper, are surrounded by the pleasures of this world, and are seemingly without a care (Ps 73:2-9), fret not. Do not look to natural man or to the world for release from your burdens (Ps 73:16-17). Instead, draw near to Me. Put all your trust in Me. Focus on Me and My eternal promises, rather than on the transient trials you now face (Ps 73:28). Put aside the foolishness of comparing your current situation with that of those around you. Instead, I want you to trust that, in the end, I will make all things right.

My precious one, I want you to continue to run the good race (Heb 12:1-2), storing up for yourself treasures in heaven where moths and rust cannot destroy (Mt 6:19-21).

I know it is tempting to question My love for you when you find yourself walking through the valley (Ps 23:4). I know it is tempting to blame yourself, wondering if you have somehow failed in your faith. So many times I have heard My precious children utter the words, "If I only had more faith, I wouldn't be experiencing such difficulty." Listen, My love, you live in a fallen world where Satan has temporary domain (Jn 12:31, 14:30). As a result, there is pain, suffering, and sorrow.

Think upon My Son of whom it is written, "a Man of sorrows, and acquainted with grief" (Isa 53:3). Do you believe His sorrows were the result of faltering faith? Of course not! Yet He experienced weariness (Jn 4:6), distress (Lk 12:50), anger, grief (Mk 3:5), and great trouble and unrest (Jn 12:27). He experienced trials, temptations (Lk 4:1-2), and persecutions to the point of death on a cross (Lk 22:63-64, Php 2:8); all this suffering, and none of it due to a lack of faith (2 Co 5:21).

My child, in this world you will have trials (1 Pe 4:12-13), but I am your portion. Stand strong in the face of adversity (Eph 6:13-18). Remember that all your trials and afflictions are temporary (2 Co 4:16-18). Do not forget that I am a God of justice (Ps 89:14), and that everything will be made right in eternity, for eternity. Beloved, I promise that I will personally wipe away all your tears (Rev 7:17). So do not give up. Refuse to give *Me* up. Be patient and wait (Lam 3:25-26); I promise your reward will be great.

Are You Willing To Run?

Let us lay aside every weight, and the sin which so easily ensnares us, and let us run with endurance the race that is set before us, looking unto Jesus, the author and finisher of our faith, who for the joy that was set before Him endured the cross, despising the shame, and has sat down at the right hand of the throne of God.
Heb 12:1-2

My dear child, I want you to discipline and train your mind and body, just as a world-class athlete disciplines and trains for a big race (1 Co 9:24-27). You must focus, like an athlete, on the goal—the Prize—which is not only meeting Me face to face in eternity, but also living the abundant life here and now (Jn 10:10).

Think about everything the athlete endures in order to run a good race—daily workouts, self-discipline, self-denial, and perseverance. The athlete often gives up comfort, ease, time, and a myriad of unhealthy habits, in which many non-athletes frequently indulge and thoroughly enjoy. The result is stamina, character, strength, health, and even joy in the running. Many may think the athlete's curious, disciplined lifestyle is devoid of too many of the pleasures of life. However, what they do not understand or experience is the sheer exhilaration of a race well run. And, sadly, they never experience the joy of obtaining the Prize.

Are you willing to run in such a race? Are you willing to endure hardship as a good soldier of Jesus Christ (2 Ti 2:3-5)? Are you willing to follow His example? Are you willing to set aside your agenda and acknowledge Me in all your ways? Are you willing to allow Me to direct your paths (Pr 3:6-7)? Are you willing to die to your own flesh and instead live by the Spirit (Ro 8:13)?

Do not give in to the temptation to first bury your dead before you decide to follow Me. Instead, determine to make Me your first loyalty in everything you do (Mt 8:21-22). I must be more important to you than television, entertainment, hobbies, career, home, and even family (Mt 10:37). Lay down your idols. Determine to have no other gods before Me (Ex 20:3), and love Me with all your heart, soul, and mind (Mt 22:37).

Know this, My beloved: The crown of blessing for running the race is yours now—given to you as you compete. You do not have to wait for the final victory to receive My blessing. The very fact that you are running within the context of My will is the victory right here and now: This is the abundant life. This is My kingdom on earth.

So come, My beloved, and run with Me on the path I have chosen for you. And rejoice, knowing that all My plans are for your benefit and are better than anything you could possibly imagine (Jer 29:11, Jn 10:10).

*I have come
That they might have life,
And that they
May have it more
Abundantly.*
John 10:10

Know The Joy Of Submitting To My Authority

Take My yoke upon you and learn from Me, for I am gentle and lowly in heart, and you will find rest for your souls.
Mt 11:29

My precious child, there is no reason to fear My authority—My instructions, guidance, commands, or calling on your life. I want you to understand that there is no need to bristle and chafe against My will for you at any time.

There may have been those in your life who abused their authority over you. Maybe they gave you tasks that were too difficult and demanding, then treated you harshly when you failed. Or maybe you experienced unkind, thoughtless authorities who failed to acknowledge your feelings or your worth. Beloved, do not let those experiences with authority figures pollute your understanding of the nature of My authority in your life (Hos 11:4, Mk 10:42-45).

You need not fear that you will not measure up to My call on your life. And I want you to set aside all beliefs that I am a harsh, uncaring, unforgiving taskmaster just waiting for you to err. On the contrary, I promise I will give you everything you need to accomplish My will (Php 4:13, 2 Pe 1:3); I promise that nothing can separate you from My love (Ro 8:38-39); I promise that My grace is sufficient in all your weaknesses and failings (2 Co 12:9); I promise that when you fall I will lovingly scoop you into My arms (Ps 37:23-24); and I promise that I will willingly and gladly forgive all your sins (1 Jn 1:8-9).

If you start to fear or resent My authority, remind yourself that submitting to Me leads to joy and abundant life (Ps 16:11, Jn 10:10, 15:9-11). And remember that My authority over you cannot be separated from My servant's heart toward you. For though I have authority over you, I also humbly and gently became your Servant (Mt 20:26-28).

Remember My great love for you (1 Jn 3:1, 1 Jn 4:9-10): For your sake, I willingly humbled Myself and became as a slave, obedient to the point of death on a cross. Know that I did all this out of love for you and for the hope and joy of spending eternity with you (Php 2:7-8, Jn 3:16). Now do you see that, because of My sacrificial love, there is no need to fear My authority?

The truth is, you will find peace and rest for your soul *only* under My yoke of authority. That is because I am your Counselor and your Prince of Peace (Isa 9:6). Finally, I want you to remember My promise that, when you obey and submit to My authority, you will know the fullness of joy (Jn 15:9-11).

Receive My Love,
Then Pass It On To Others

Behold what manner of love the Father has bestowed on us, that we should be called children of God!
1 Jn 3:1

My beloved child, I want you to know the astonishing depth of My continual love for you. I want you to know that I love you in *every* situation in your life. I want you to receive My boundless love when you're having a good day—joyfully following Me on the path I have chosen for you. And I want you to receive My love when you're having a bad day—choosing to rebel instead of following My lead: I meant it when I told you that *nothing* can separate you from My love (Ro 8:38-39), not even your disobedience—not even when you are at your worst.

You may be changing from one day, even one moment, to the next, but I *never* change (Heb 13:8). For instance, you may be loving and obeying Me in a particular moment and thus pleased with yourself as you walk with Me. Consequently, you feel you have earned and deserve My love. That's when it's easy for you to receive My love. However, I want you to know that you're equally loved when you are sinning against Me: My love for you is constant and unchanging, and there is nothing you can do to earn it (Gal 2:16, Eph 2:4-5, 8-9). My love is a free, unearned gift, and the only reason you are able to love Me is because I first loved you (1 Jn 4:19). You don't have to *do* anything to win My love and acceptance. I simply love you because that's My character: It's who I am (1 Jn 4:8). It's what I do, and that will never change, because I never change.

So you see, My beloved, there is nothing you have ever done, or ever can do, to earn or to keep My love: It just *is.* That means you can be experiencing your darkest moments of defiance, sin, rebellion, and hate, yet, I simply respond by saying, "I love you." I do not change, and My love for you does not change: that's just the way it is.

So the next time you're feeling particularly vile, I love you. The next time you decide to rebel, I love you. The next time you utterly fail, I love you: I *am* love (1 Jn 4:8). So receive My love. This is My gift to you which will never be taken away (Ps 100:5, 103:17, Jer 31:3).

Remember, I laid all your sins, rebellion, and failure upon My Son. I punished Him for your transgressions. He paid the price. He suffered so that you could have peace (Isa 53:5-6). Do you believe I didn't punish Him enough? Is that why there's a part of you that still thinks I will punish you in addition to how I punished My Son? Is that why you insist on punishing yourself? Remember, My Son bore *all* your sins (Isa 53:11). He also bore *all* the punishment for your sins. Why then do you insist on believing I still want or need to punish you?

Do you see that I'm inviting you to see Me for who I really am rather than what you expect and believe that I am? I am *not* a condemning, punishing God. Rather, I am the One who has made full provision for you so that you are not condemned, but saved. *I am the One who loves you all the time, no matter what* (Ro 8:31-35). I want you to live and move and breathe in this truth, walking continuously in My love for you. I also want you to know that the wealth of love I continuously lavish on you is the same love I lavish on *all* people, whether they believe in and obey Me or not.

Do not be like the Pharisees who criticized My Son for associating with the outcasts of society (Lk 15:1-2). Do not fall into the trap of believing My love is only for those who are righteous: I so loved the *world*—not just those who believe and follow Me—that I gave My Son (Jn 3:16). The delineation between those who believe and those who do not believe comes only at the end of this age when I decide who will live with Me for eternity. Until then, *all* are dearly loved with no condemnation (Jn 3:17).

Jesus came to embrace sinners (Mt 9:12-13) and to love them (Jn 13:34). He came to reveal the love of the Father—My love, for *all* people. He perfectly mirrored My love, grace, and heart for the world. I love everyone. I love everyone. *I love everyone!* My arms are open wide, longing for *all* to enter in. I do not want to lose a single precious soul (2 Pt 3:9).

Are you starting to understand the depths of My wondrous love? Do you see that you cannot escape My love? Do you see that My love is the same for all people, and that I long to embrace everyone in My arms?

So receive My great, mysterious, deep, wonderful, and unending love, beloved. Then, tell others who do not yet know, so they will receive as well and run into My arms.

I Am Still Involved

But, beloved, do not forget this one thing, that with the Lord one day is as a thousand years, and a thousand years as one day. The Lord is not slack concerning His promise, as some count slackness, but is longsuffering toward us, not willing that any should perish but that all should come to repentance.
2 Pt 3:8-9

Are you fearful or angry with Me for not intervening in the wickedness and suffering you see in the world? I understand. But in spite of all the wickedness and suffering you see, I am still involved.

Let Me remind you that I discipline those I love (Heb 12:6-7). After all, what happens to a child whose parents refuse to discipline? She becomes spoiled, unpleasant to be near, selfish, demanding, and unruly. Interestingly, she also feels unloved because she senses her parents did not care enough to set appropriate limits. Beloved, I am your heavenly Father who loves the world enough to use discipline when necessary. This is why I allow the world to experience the consequences of disobeying Me. Think about it. Would I give My own Son to suffer and die for humankind (Ro 8:32) and then neglect the need for discipline? Absolutely not!

Remember, however, that My discipline is designed to remind the world of Me and My ways (Ps 119:71-72, 92): it is designed to teach people that My instructions for living are right, superior, good, and produce blessing (Ps 119:165-176). I use the natural consequences of sin to discipline and thus woo people back into My loving arms. I do this by allowing people to experience the trials that result from disobedience and the blessings that result from obedience.

This does not mean, however, that when you obey Me you will never experience trials. After all, Jesus suffered greatly because of the sin around Him. But He also experienced the greatest blessing of all: He walked in daily intimacy with Me. I want everyone to experience the same intimacy, strength, peace, joy, and love that Jesus did—even in the midst of trials. It is possible to be blessed, even in the midst of great suffering. Now do you see that I allow trials and suffering because I want My wayward children to come to Me?

Remember also that I give My beloved children the choice to love and obey Me. If I remove this choice what would happen? If I step in every time someone is about to disobey Me and do evil against someone else, there would be no *real* free choice, and there would be no *real* love for Me. Love that is commanded, coerced, manipulated, or controlled is not love at all.

I could become like a cosmic policeman and prevent all evil. However, this would mean you would suddenly be living in a robot-like world where things would happen automatically and mechanically. In this scenario you would lose all your freedom to love Me and others in a deep and meaningful way. I don't want that for My creation. And I know that in your heart, you don't want that either. I want you to be free to *really* live and to *really* love. I want love and obedience from you that is freely, joyfully, and sincerely given. Isn't that what you want from those who love you?

Having the ability to freely choose love, however, means that people must also have the ability to freely choose hate. And there are consequences for each choice. Your choice to love and obey Me, or to refuse to love and obey, will be honored. I take this freedom to choose very seriously—so much so, that the choice you make now will be honored for eternity. But, in My grace and love, I am waiting to pronounce final judgment, hoping and wanting that more of My precious children will choose Me. This is why I do not stop all evil now. I want everyone to have the opportunity to freely choose to love and to spend eternity with Me.

So you see, My child, I am still involved in the world, no matter how dark things may appear; I promise that I am with you always, even to the end of the age (Mt 28:20); I promise that I will never leave you nor forsake you (Heb 13:5). Remember, I do not will this evil you see around you, but I will use it for a greater good (Ro 8:28), wooing My precious ones back into My loving arms. In My arms they will find rest and peace (Isa 26:3)—even in the midst of trials and suffering.

For I know the thoughts that I think toward you, says the LORD, thoughts of peace and not of evil, to give you a future and a hope. Then you will call upon Me and go and pray to Me, and I will listen to you. And you will seek Me and find Me, when you search for Me with all your heart. I will be found by you, says the LORD ... (Jer 29:11-14): this is My promise to you, beloved.

Choose Me

And if it seems evil to you to serve the Lord, choose for yourselves this day whom you will serve ... but as for me and my house, we will serve the Lord.
Jos 24:15

Beloved, I want you to be aware of all the choices you make in a day. Do you realize you are choosing to serve either Me or the enemy with the decisions you make? O that you would slow down and ask yourself whom you are choosing to serve as you go about your day.

Is the world beckoning you with its attractive ways? Remember, I have called you to be in the world but not of it (Jn 17:14-16). Whom do you choose this day, this very moment? Do you see that I ask you *whom* do you choose rather than *what* do you choose? This is because I want you to realize that you are not only choosing, for example, between watching a violent television program and going for a walk. Rather, the real choice you are making is whether you are going to serve the enemy or Me. Now do you see why the decisions you make are so important?

The world's ways can be so tempting: "It's just a television show," you tell yourself. But I tell you that your decision runs deeper than that. Remember, those who love Me obey Me (Jn 14:21). So, when you are choosing to watch that television program, *whom*, not just *what*, are you choosing to love?

Do you want more of My manifest presence in your life? I am giving you the key: The one who obeys Me, loves Me. And he is the one who receives a greater awareness of My loving, tender presence (Jn 15:9-11). He is also the one who, with each decision to serve Me, grows in love, joy, peace, patience, kindness, goodness, faithfulness, gentleness, and self-control; those who are Mine resist the sinful passions and desires of this world (Gal 5:18-24). These are the ones who understand that to gain the world and all its pleasures is a complete and utter loss when compared to the price of losing Me (Mk 8:36). Are you counting the cost of your daily decisions?

Am I saying you lose your salvation when you sin? Of course not! Remember, My beloved Son has made it possible for you to come boldly before My throne of grace (Eph 2:13). And I am faithful to forgive when you confess and repent of your sins (1 Jn 1:9). However, unconfessed, persistent, and unrepentant sin separates you from Me (Isa 59:2). You see, I came into the world that you might have life and have it more abundantly (Jn 10:10). I *am* the life (Jn 14:6). So, when you make decisions to sin, serving the enemy rather than Me, you become separated from Me—the very source of abundance, peace, joy, love, life, and all that is good (Jas 1:17).

Do you want to experience more of the joy of My abiding presence? Then choose this day whom you will serve. Do not turn from Me causing Me to hide My face from you for even a moment (Dt 31:18). But, when you sin, quickly confess and turn from that sin so that you may once again experience the One who is life itself.

*Then I will sprinkle
Clean water on you,
And you will be clean ...
I will give you a new heart
With new and right desires,
And I will put a new spirit in you.
I will take out your stony heart of sin
And give you a new, obedient heart....
You will be My people,
And I will be your God.*
Ezekiel 36:25-26, 28

Faith Without Works Is Dead

Was not Abraham our Father justified by works when he offered Isaac his son on the altar? Do you see that faith was working together with his works, and by works faith was made perfect? And the scripture was fulfilled which says, "Abraham believed God, and it was accounted to him for righteousness." And he was called the friend of God.
Jas 2:21-23

My beloved, do you see that works are not limited to acts of service? Do you see that at the heart of any good and pleasing work is a faithful and obedient heart that responds to My calling and direction? You see, My love, works are simply acts of obedience. Abraham was not serving anyone but Me when he offered his son on the altar. Yet, I counted his obedience as a good work.

Satan, however, perverts the idea of works. He tries to deceive My children with the lie that good works consist only of labor, service to others, and activity. His hope is to distract you from a rich, deep relationship with Me by keeping you perpetually busy. He knows that spending time with Me in intimate stillness is essential for maintaining a deep and powerful connection—and there is nothing he wants more than to prevent you from walking in powerful connection with Me.

So, My child, you must learn to recognize My voice and obey Me when I tell you to spend quiet time with Me. Obedience is obedience. It does not matter whether I'm calling you to slow down and be still, or telling you to serve Me in a more active and visible manner; your choice to obey Me is counted unto you as a good work.

Notice that Abraham was not giving money to the poor, helping in the church kitchen, or volunteering for any other good and necessary task. He was simply responding to My directions. He was walking in obedience. He listened to My voice, walked with Me by his side, and trusted in My faithfulness, goodness, love, and wisdom. How could I not call him friend, this man who so completely trusted and obeyed Me, even to the point of offering his one and only son?

Won't you give Me that same trust? How I long for you to walk beside Me, perfecting your faith with the good works of trust and obedience.

So come, My beloved. Listen for My voice. Experience the fullness of joy that results from obedience to My call (Jn 15:9-11). Hear Me call you "friend" as I make known to you My will (Jn 15:14-15). Resist the compulsion to remain perpetually busy. Resist the lie that activity is the only thing that pleases Me. Know that I am well pleased by your every work of trust and obedience—no matter how small or how great.

Look Unto Me

I tell you the truth, the Son can do nothing by Himself; He can do only what He sees His Father doing, because whatever the Father does the Son also does. For the Father loves the Son and shows Him all He does.
Jn 5:19-20, NIV

My beloved, be careful not to let yourself be distracted—not even with good things. Instead, determine to seek Me first and thus learn to walk in a peaceful, abundant, and satisfying relationship with Me. Remember, even My precious Son did nothing but what I showed Him.

Too many of My children are in a hurry to serve Me without inquiring when, where, and how I want them to serve (Ps 127:1). Do not believe the lie that you have to fill your time with constant activity in order to serve in My kingdom. I'm not in a hurry, not even in these end times with much left to do. So, take time to incline your heart to Me, and let Me direct your paths (Ps 32:8, 73:24).

"In returning and rest you shall be saved; in quietness and confidence shall be your strength" (Isa 30:15). I spoke these words to the Israelites as they trembled in fear, knowing the powerful Assyrians were about to launch an attack against them. However, rather than returning to My arms and listening quietly and confidently to My instructions, they decided to act independently of Me and My will. The result was disastrous (Isa 30:1, 16-17, 31:1-3).

I promise to guide and lead you in all your ways (Pr 3:5-6). So won't you let Me direct you in the ways in which I want you to work for My kingdom? Just think how fruitless it would have been had Moses decided of his own accord that he was going to help decrease the Israelites' suffering in Egypt. He could have easily reasoned that persuading Pharaoh to allow him to build better homes for the Israelite slaves was a good idea. After all, there was an obvious need (Pr 12:15, 14:12).

Do you see how important it is to seek Me and know My will, even in deciding how to work for My kingdom? How tragic it would have been had Moses not paid attention to or obeyed My instructions. He could have struggled in his own strength, occupying all his time and energy with building houses—all the while *not* working in accordance with My good and perfect will. Had he gone ahead with his own ideas, he would have missed the greatest opportunity of his life—experiencing a personal relationship with Me.

He would have missed knowing and walking with Me in ways he never could have imagined (Eph 3:20). He would have missed witnessing and experiencing My extravagant love and mighty power as I freed the Israelites from captivity (Ex 3:7-10). He would have missed meeting and conversing with Me on the top of Mt. Sinai (Ex19:19-20). He would have missed the blessing of continually dwelling with Me as I made My home among the Israelites. He also would have missed experiencing My leading with a pillar of fire by night and a cloud by day (Ex 40:34-38). He never would have tasted sweet manna from heaven (Ex 16:11-15), witnessed water pouring from rock (Ex 17:5-6), or a battle fought and won simply by raising his arms toward heaven (Ex 17:11-13). Moses never would have known that I had so much more in store for him than building houses if he wouldn't have sought Me first.

Do you see why I rejoice when My children listen to and obey Me rather than pursue their own agenda for advancing My kingdom?

So, My child, you must learn to discern whether or not an assignment is from Me. Ask Me to show you when and if you are responding to a need without having received My call. You also must remember, even when you are called, that if you run ahead of Me, take your eyes off Me, or try to do the assignment without Me at your side, your peace will suffer (Isa 26:3).

So lean into Me as never before. Be wise, and persistently seek Me and My will (Mt 6:33). If you become harried or stressed, come to Me. Ask if I have called you to bear the burden you are carrying. And remember to remain yoked to Me while carrying any burden which I have given you. My yoke is easy and My burden is light (Mt 11:30). So, the key is staying under My yoke and walking hand in hand with Me. There you will receive an abundance of grace and strength to do all things (Ro 8:32, Php 4:13).

Do Not Settle For Less Than Me

And behold, the LORD passed by, and a great and strong wind tore into the mountains and broke the rocks in pieces before the LORD, but the LORD was not in the wind; and after the wind an earthquake, but the LORD was not in the earthquake; and after the earthquake a fire, but the LORD was not in the fire; and after the fire a still small voice. So it was, when Elijah heard it, that he wrapped his face in his mantle and went out and stood in the entrance of the cave. Suddenly a voice came to him, and said, "What are you doing here, Elijah?"
1Ki 19:11-13

My beloved child, do not be so distracted by religious forms and traditions that you miss *Me*. Do not settle for comfortable rituals thinking that, by participating in these activities, you have heard My voice and met and walked with Me. Do not be like the Pharisees who proudly strutted their religious knowledge, works, and righteousness while neglecting and even hating Me (Mt 23:5-7, 13-15).

I want you to go beyond religion—beyond that which is easy to see and do (Hos 6:6). I want you to look beyond the wind, the earthquake, and the fire. I want you to listen for My still small voice. Sitting in a church pew every Sunday is not My still small voice. Volunteering on a committee is not My still small voice. Giving to the poor is not My still small voice. Tithing is not My still small voice. Even reading the Bible is not My still small voice when you value the Word of the LORD more highly than the LORD of the Word.

My still small voice is heard by those who look beyond the wind, the earthquake, and the fire. It's heard by those who wait upon Me, long for Me, and desire to meet with Me in the beauty of a loving relationship. My sheep know My voice (Jn 10:4-5), and I want all My children to know My voice—not just the sounds of the wind and the fire. Do you see the difference, My precious one? O how I long to draw all My beloved children into sweet rapport with Me.

I tell you to seek, and you shall find (Lk 11:9-10). My beloved, are you truly seeking or have you simply settled for participating in lesser experiences? Listen, can you hear Me calling? Look beyond. Go deeper. Go further. Do not be so enamored with the wind and the fire that you miss the *Creator* of the wind and the fire.

Do not settle for less than Me. Do not even settle for reflections of Me, or for that which I use for My glory. I say it again; do not settle for less than Me. No one enters My kingdom or sees the Father but by *Me* (Jn 14:6). My dear child, you cannot enter My kingdom through going to church, volunteering, or giving. You may only enter because you know and obey Me, and because I know you (Mt 7:21-23). Do you see why it is so important to refuse to settle for less than Me?

Do you hear Me calling, My beloved? It's your LORD. Come; wrap yourself in humility and obedience. Rise up out of the cave. Hear Me ask, "What are you doing here?" Then, walk hand in hand with Me into the light.

My Heart's Desire

You shall love the Lord your God with all your heart, with all your soul, and with all your mind.
Mt 22:37

My beloved, My heart's desire is that you love Me. It's that simple—and it's that profound. Do you love Me with all that you have, with all that you do, and with all that you are? For this is the greatest commandment. It's My heart's deepest desire, and it's the very reason you were created.

Hear My heart, My child: My desire to walk with you in a loving relationship is so great that I sent My only Son to die a terrible death on your behalf (Jn 3:16). I want to reveal Myself to you, and I want to make My home with you (Jn 14:23). This is My heart's desire. Will you respond?

It's not enough to know *about* Me. Even Satan knows about Me and enters My presence upon occasion (Job 1:6). It's not enough to know My Word. Even Satan knows My Word (Mt 4:5-6). It's not enough to be circumcised in body while ignoring the spirit—making outward shows of love and devotion while not truly loving Me from your heart (Jer 9:24-27). Remember, it's the pure in heart who will see Me (Mt 5:8). So respond to My heart's desire, My beloved, and give back to Me the love that I give to you (1 Jn 4:19).

I am grieved and My heart aches because there are many who are doing great exploits in My name. Yet, they do not really know Me, walk with Me, or love Me with a pure heart. These are the precious ones that will hear Me say on the great day of judgment, "I never knew you; depart from Me" (Mt 7:21-23).

Please, My child, hear My heart: Draw near to Me, and I will draw near to you (Jas 4:8). Love Me. Delight in Me (Ps 37:4). If you are not sure where to begin, read My Word, and let My Spirit lovingly speak to you through its pages. Seek fellowship with others who love Me so they can encourage you and model how to walk with Me in deep and rewarding love.

Examine your heart, My beloved. Repent of any false show of love that lacks the authenticity and sincerity of a pure heart. Ask for a pure heart of love and devotion, for I am the Giver of all good gifts (Jas 1:17). Know that I am your adoring Father whose love for you is profound beyond knowledge (Eph 3:18-19). Seek Me, and you will find Me—but you need to seek (Lk 11:9). Ask, and I will surely give—but you need to ask (Lk 11:10-13). Remember, you have not because you ask not (Jas 4:2).

So take time, My beloved, to look into your heart. Put aside all false displays of love and devotion. And allow Me to transform your heart as you focus on My beauty and receive My love (2 Co 3:18).

Do Not Settle Into The Status Quo

For the kingdom of heaven is like a man traveling to a far country, who called his own servants and delivered his goods to them. And to one he gave five talents, to another two, and to another one, to each according to his own ability; and immediately he went on a journey. Then he who had received the five talents went and traded with them, and made another five talents. And likewise he who had received two gained two more also. But he who had received one went and dug in the ground, and hid his lord's money.... So he who had received five talents came and brought five other talents, saying, 'Lord, you delivered to me five talents; look, I have gained five more talents besides them.' His lord said to him, 'Well done, good and faithful servant; you were faithful over a few things, I will make you ruler over many things. Enter into the joy of your lord'.... Then he who had received the one talent came and said, 'Lord ... I was afraid and went and hid your talent in the ground. Look, there you have what is yours.' But his lord answered and said to him, 'You wicked and lazy servant ... take the talent from him, and give it to him who has ten talents. For to everyone who has, more will be given, and he will have abundance; but from him who does not have, even what he has will be taken away.'
Mt 25:14-18, 20-21, 24-26, 28-29

*B*eloved, this parable is not only about being a good steward of your material blessings, it's also about being a good steward of our relationship and the work I am doing within you. It includes the admonition to continually grow in your walk with Me. And it's a warning against choosing to bury what you have—remaining comfortably satisfied with the status quo. I want you to grow closer and closer to Me everyday. I want you to walk in greater and greater revelation of who I am. I want you to become more and more like Me with each passing day. So, do not settle for the status quo in our relationship or in your current level of spiritual maturity.

I want all My children to understand that I am a God of transformation (2 Co 3:18, Php 1:6). I am changing you from glory into glory, and I will continue to change you from glory into glory. But, in order for Me to do this, you need to cooperate. How can I build upon what I have already given you if you are not interested in continuing the building process? Do not succumb to satisfaction with your current level of maturity or with your current relationship with Me, for there is always more.

Do you notice that the lord's servants in this parable needed to put forth effort in order to increase their master's yield? Beloved, I want you to invest everything I have given you materially, relationally, and spiritually so that I can give you even more. I want you to be responsible with the little you have, so that I can entrust you with more.

Remember, I am an infinite God, and there are a multitude of mysteries, wonders, and blessings yet to experience. All you need to do is choose to continue growing rather than remaining content with the status quo. O, how I long for you to continue to grow.

Remember Enoch (Gen 5:23-24)? He was a man who refused to settle for the status quo. He stayed close to Me. He continually remained open to more transformation and to a closer and closer walk with Me. He carefully stewarded everything I gave him and never settled into complacent satisfaction. He could have chosen to stop growing. After all, he had a great relationship with Me and was blessed. Instead, he chose to invest—build upon everything I had given him, drawing closer and closer to Me until he literally slipped into heaven!

So press in, My child, and then press in for more. When you find yourself waning in your desire to press in and grow further, ask Me for more hunger and more desire. Remember, you have not because you ask not (Jas 4:2). So ask, My love, for it is My good pleasure to give you My kingdom (Lk 12:32). Ask and press in. Ask and invest. Ask and grow. Do not bury what you have—do not become satisfied and complacent. Do not settle for the status quo. Remember, I am the One who is doing the good work of growth and transformation within you. All you need to do is steward well what I am already doing. Then you will hear Me say, "Well done, good and faithful servant. Enter into the joy of your LORD" (Mt 25:21).

*Your faith
And hope
Are in
God.*
1 Peter 1:21

What Are You Clinging To?

I am the true vine.... Abide in Me, and I in you. As the branch cannot bear fruit of itself, unless it abides in the vine, neither can you, unless you abide in Me. I am the vine, you are the branches. He who abides in Me, and I in him, bears much fruit; for without Me you can do nothing.
Jn 15:1, 4-5

My beloved, I want to remind you that when you are feeling unsatisfied, undernourished, or unfulfilled, you need to turn to Me and cling to Me all the more closely; I am the only true vine for you, My precious branch.

I want you to remember that when you choose to seek, cling to, or attach yourself to counterfeit vines, you will suffer from malnourishment causing you to feel unsatisfied and unfulfilled. For I am the bread of life (Jn 6:48), and I am life itself (Jn 14:6). Therefore, in order to be fully satisfied, you must cling to Me rather than attaching yourself to any counterfeit vine that only appears to offer life. Remember, it is only as you abide in Me that you will enjoy an abundant, full, satisfying life (Jn 6:33, 47, 51, 10:10).

Do not fall into the trap of believing you will be happy and fulfilled when you get that job promotion, when you are making more money, when you have a larger ministry, when you are driving a nicer car, or when you are living in a larger house. Do not cling to the vines of entertainment and pleasure hoping they will satisfy you. Do not even look to your loved ones for fulfillment because clinging to *any* vine other than Me will end in malnourishment, disappointment, dissatisfaction, and inner emptiness.

Think upon these two vines, My child. One is vital and living with roots that are deeply anchored in nutrient-dense soil. The other vine looks alive, healthy, and even beautiful. But, it's artificial with no root system to deliver nutrients or to keep it from being blown and tossed by the wind. Which one of these vines would you rather cling to? Which vine is able to sustain your life, supplying you with nourishment and the ability to produce fruit? Which vine has the ability to keep you anchored during the storms of life?

My beloved, cling to Me, your True Vine. Cling to Me in your weariness and emptiness, and I will satisfy you; I will give you rest (Mt 11:28-30). Do not cling to counterfeit vines that will starve you and rob you of the ability to bear fruit (Mk 4:18-19). But seek Me first, My precious child. Cling to Me, and everything else will be added unto you (Mt 6:33).

Seek Not The Kingdom Of This World

Do not lay up for yourselves treasures on earth, where moth and rust destroy and where thieves break in and steal; but lay up for yourselves treasures in heaven where neither moth nor rust destroy and where thieves do not break in and steal. For where your treasure is, there your heart will be also.
Mt 6:19-21
Jesus answered, "My kingdom is not of this world."
Jn 18:36

*B*eloved, do not succumb to the spirit of the world that entices My children to seek only that which they can see with the natural eye and experience with the flesh; I promise so much more than what the world has to offer: I promise there is nothing you have seen or will see on earth that compares with that which I have prepared for you in My kingdom (Jn 14:2-3). You cannot even begin to imagine the beauty and joy that awaits you (1 Co 2:9)!

Die to your fleshly desires (Ro 8:5), My precious child, and seek Me and My kingdom (Mt 6:33). Do you notice that when you focus on worldly possessions, your desire quickly turns toward all things material? Do you notice how you begin to feel unrest and discontentment as your desire for that which pleases your flesh intensifies? This is a trap, My beloved, from which I want you to be completely free. For freedom and true contentment are found only in delighting yourself in Me (Ps 37:4).

Remember that as you focus on Me, you will experience peace—even perfect peace (Isa 26:3). I also promise that when you make Me your delight, rather than the things of this world, you will receive the desires of your heart. Understand, however, that I promise you the desires of your heart, not the desires of your flesh. For, as you allow Me to do so, I will give you a new heart that longs for Me (Ez 36:25-27). I will give you a heart that turns away from all your former idols. You will no longer hunger for more and more material wealth. You will no longer seek notoriety, the praises of men, power, or influence. For I am the LORD, and you shall have no other gods before Me (Ex 20:3). If you will turn to Me, you will be Mine, and I will be yours (Ez 36:28b). And I promise that when you turn to Me, you will know no greater joy (Ps 16:11, 144:15b, 146:5).

So turn your eyes away from the enchantments of this world, My precious child, and look upon Me—the Source of all that is good (Jas 1:17), meaningful, and lasting (1 Ti 1:17). Make Me your treasure. Only when *I* have become your treasure have you truly given Me your heart (Mt 6:21), and your heart is what I require (Mt 22:37-38).

What Do You Seek?

But seek first the kingdom of God and His righteousness, and all these things shall be added to you.
Mt 6:33

*M*y child, are you seeking Me first as a person, or are you more excited about My gifts, blessings, and benefits? O, how I long for you to taste and see that *I* am good (Ps 34:8). How I long for you to experience the blessing of loving *Me* more than the gifts I have to offer; there is no want for those who seek *Me* (Ps 34:9). So you must learn to distinguish the difference between seeking and wanting more of Me—desiring a closer relationship with Me—and wanting only My gifts: My guidance, knowledge, wisdom, protection, and provision—merely the tangible benefits of an association with Me.

Which is better, marrying someone who is wealthy because you want to have the benefits of their wealth, or marrying someone you deeply love and then realizing your new spouse has wealth he is eager to share? Likewise, I want My children to love Me for Me—not because they want what I have to offer.

From the beginning of time, My desire has been to walk side by side with My children, enjoying each other's company (Ge 3:8-9). So, do not hide yourself from Me or seek to bypass Me in pursuit of My wealth. After all, isn't that what Adam and Eve did when they sought the knowledge of good and evil rather than choosing to walk in obedience with Me (Ge 3:6)? Beloved, instead of pursuing only My blessings, come into My presence, into the Holy of Holies, and experience sweet communion with Me.

Let Me remind you, there is no need to struggle to enter into My presence; I have torn, from the top downward, the veil that once separated Me from you (Mt 27:51). Therefore, it is not necessary for you to try to tear, from the bottom upward, that which I have already done. For lo, I am with you always—even to the end of the age (Mt 28:20b). So, you do not need to struggle to be with Me; I'm already continually with you.

I want you to be so enamored with Me that everything within you wants to bless My holy name (Ps 103:1). I want you to be so caught up in enjoying Me that you exclaim, "O, in the midst of praising You for who You are, I almost forgot to praise You for all You've done" (Ps 103:2-5). Do you see the difference? Do you see the shift in focus and desire?

So ask Me to reveal to you when you are straying from the pure desire to walk with Me. For what loving, earthly father would, when his child asks for a piece of bread, give him a stone instead (Mt 7:7-11)? How much more will I, your heavenly Father, give to you that which is good? I say to you, I will certainly respond to your heartfelt request to seek Me first. Nothing would please Me more.

Come To Me

Come to Me, all you who labor and are heavy laden, and I will give you rest. Take My yoke upon you and learn from Me, for I am gentle and lowly in heart, and you will find rest for your souls. For My yoke is easy and My burden is light.
Mt 11:28-29

My precious one, I know there are times when you look at your busy, hectic life and wonder how you can possibly accomplish everything you feel you need to do. I know there are times when you are stressed by the weight of multiple responsibilities. Beloved, I want to relieve you of your heavy burdens and give you My rest. All you need to do is come to Me. That's right, My love; just come to Me. I am calling you to take your eyes off your own life and its busyness and put all your trust in Me (2 Sa 22:3, 7, 17-20, 31, 33).

Do you realize that when you feel stressed, you have taken your eyes off Me and My sufficiency, choosing instead to trust in your own abilities and efforts? Remember, it is possible to remain in perfect peace in spite of your circumstances (Isa 26:3-4, Php 4:11-13). I am not saying this to condemn or shame you. Instead, I want to encourage and remind you that there is great power and peace for those who remain in Me. However, apart from Me, you can do nothing (Jn 15:5).

Now do you see that the stress you often feel is due to the fact that you try to live aspects of your life without My help and guidance? Rejoice, My dear one, for now the presence of stress will serve as a reminder for you to call upon Me, turn to Me, and trust Me.

I promise I will give you everything you need (Mt 6:25-34, Php 4:19). So come to Me. I want you to commit everything you do to Me, trusting Me, and I *will* help you (Ps 37:5). Do not be anxious about anything. Instead, come to Me, abide in Me, walk with Me, and tell Me all your wants and needs. I promise that, in so doing, you will experience My peace (Php 4:6-7).

Your whole life is meant to be lived in My courts (Ps 27:4), *dwelling* in My presence—not just visiting Me upon occasion (Ps 91:1-2). This is My heart's desire, My precious one. *Dwell* with Me. Come to Me. I am gentle and loving, and I long to embrace you with an everlasting embrace that promises to calm you in the midst of life's storms.

So come to Me, My precious one, even in the midst of all your busyness, and know My peace (Jn 14:27).

*I am my
Beloved's,
And my beloved
Is mine.*
Song of Solomon 6:3

Be Yourself

O Lord, You have searched me and known me. You know my sitting down and my rising up; You understand my thoughts afar off. You comprehend my path and my lying down, and are acquainted with all my ways. For there is not a word on my tongue, but behold, O Lord, You know it altogether. You have hedged me behind and before, and laid Your hand upon me. Such knowledge is too wonderful for me; it is high, I cannot attain it.
Ps 139:1-6

*B*eloved, do you know how highly I value you and all that makes you unique? I know your every thought, desire, dream, and quirk; I know you even better than you know yourself—and I love you and delight in you (Ps 149:4a). Just think, *I am the One who values you with My own life* and calls you friend (Jn 3:16-17, Jn 15:13, 1 Jn 3:16).

So, stop trying so hard to be someone you're not, because, My friend, *I love you just the way you are.* How I grieve when you do not see the value of your own individuality and when you try to squelch the very uniqueness in which I delight (1 Co 12:4-6). You are fearfully and wonderfully made (Ps 139:14). So rejoice, My beloved, for there is no reason to try to be what you are not.

This also means that you can set aside any inkling of belief that I am a God who wants to smother the life out of you by insisting you become like a clone—monochromatic in behavior and personality; I am the One who delights in you as an individual. I formed your inward parts, lovingly watching over you in your mother's womb, calling you "marvelous" (Ps 139:13).

I love you and cherish you, and I encourage you to be *you*—the unique and wonderful individual I created you to be (1 Co 12:7-11). After all, I made you according to My specifications (Ge 1:26, 31), with the ability to fulfill your unique purpose through Me (Eph 2:10, 1 Co 3:5-6).

So come, My friend, and bless Me with a wonderful delight—you, walking by My side, becoming all that I uniquely created you to be (2 Ti 1:9).

All That Is Beautiful

Every good gift and every perfect gift is from above, and comes down from the Father of lights....
Jas 1:17

I love it, My child, when you enjoy the beauty that surrounds you: the stars; the moon; majestic mountain peaks; waltzing rivers; playful, melodic song birds; fragrant, colorful flowers; rain softly pattering.

If you were the only person on earth, I would have made all this for you alone to enjoy. How I love to surround you with beautiful gifts (Lk 12:32).

You are a beautiful, priceless gift that I have given to Myself (Eph 1:4-5, Col 1:19-20). I personally have bought you with that which is priceless—My own blood (Col 1:13-14). Do you see, now, how much I value being near you?

So won't you bless Me, this day, with the gift of your beautiful presence? How I love your gaze upon My face, your whispers in My ear, and your hand in Mine. Remember, My love, it is for the joy of being with you—My precious treasure—that I willingly gave My very life (Mt 6:21).

You are more beautiful to Me than all the stars in the sky, more beautiful than the highest of mountains, more beautiful than the rarest of flowers, and more refreshing to My heart than the gentlest of rains. So come, My beloved, and bless Me with your presence.

You Are My Beloved

"And it shall be, in that day," says the LORD, "That you will call Me 'My Husband,' and no longer call Me 'My Master,'".... "I will betroth you to Me forever; Yes, I will betroth you to Me in righteousness and justice, in loving kindness and mercy; I will betroth you to Me in faithfulness, and you shall know the LORD."
Hos 2:16, 19-20

Rejoice, My beloved, for I have called you to a glorious destiny, and you don't have to wait to begin walking in that calling! Remember, you are My bride and My beloved (Isa 54:5), and I want you to walk with Me in all the joy and intimacy that is found in a healthy, vibrant marriage—the sharing, laughter, conversation, companionship, faithfulness, and joy in one another's company. You were created to walk in intimacy with Me, enjoying Me as a dearly beloved husband and friend (SS 5:16). This is your calling.

I want you to know that when you look at Me, My heart is completely ravished by your gaze (SS 4:9). I am always by your side (Heb 13:5), delighting in our relationship. And I delight in you, as you give Me the love that I have first given you (1 Jn 4:19).

I tell you again, I will never leave your side. I love you so much that, to do so, would cause Me indescribable heartache (SS 7:10). Remember, I am the One who willingly sent My only begotten Son to die, so that, if you chose to love Me the way I love you, we would never have to be separated (Jn 3:16). Are you starting to understand that you really are My beloved (SS 6:3)?

How I long for you to fully know and respond to My deep desire to walk hand in hand with you throughout your day. This is the kind of relationship My precious Son had with Me while He walked on earth. He experienced such intimacy with Me that He did nothing without Me (Jn 5:19). This is what I want you to learn to walk in—even here—even now. And remember, the joy you experience as you walk in intimacy with Me now is just a dim reflection of the joy you will know when you finally meet Me face to face (1 Co 13:12-13).

So, walk with Me. Include Me in your activities throughout the day. Talk to Me. Listen for My replies. Enjoy My company. Get to know Me as the One who calls you beloved, the One who delights in your attention (SS 7:10). Ask Me for help remembering to include Me in your daily activities. I consider nothing about you, or your life, to be too mundane or irrelevant. Remember, I'm the One who loves you so much that I know how many hairs you have on your head (Mt 10:30).

I say it again, you are My beloved. And I deeply desire to walk with you, sharing in all that you are and all that you do. Won't you choose to set your desires on Me the way I have set Mine on you? For, My beloved, nothing would make Me happier.

My Treasure

For where your treasure is, there your heart will be also.
Mt 6:21

My desire, My heart, My love, My attention, and My focus is upon you, My beloved. If this were not so, why would I have sent My only Son to suffer and die for you? You have heard the story so many times, but stop for just a moment, and think again about the depths of My love for you (Ro 5:7-8). Think upon the cross, My child, and see My heart for you in My pierced and bleeding Son.

I love you so much that My desire is to be near you forever, and I gave absolutely everything I have to make that possible (Jn 3:16, Ro 6:23). I gave that which is precious beyond description—the only One worthy and able to purchase such a great and wonderful treasure (2 Co 5:21, Jn 1:29).

You are that treasure—and where *My* treasure is, there *My* heart will be also.

978-0-595-44886-9
0-595-44886-0